For Carol

AIQ
2026

The Collaborative Intelligence
That Determines Who Thrives

BY

DR. LAYLA MARTIN

AIQ 2026 *The Collaborative Intelligence That Determines Who Thrives*

By Dr. Layla Martin

Published by AIQ Ninja Publishing

ISBN: 9798305168013 First Edition: 2026

For permission requests, bulk orders, or licensing inquiries, contact: AIQ Ninja Publishing: team@aiqninja.com

Printed in the United States of America 10 9 8 7 6 5 4 3 2 1

Table of Contents

Chapter 1: The Pattern No One Noticed

T he numbers appeared ordinary at first. Columns of data tracking chess matches between humans and machines. Eighteen years of tournament results, stretching from 2005 to 2023. Over six thousand matches. More than two thousand players. The kind of dataset that usually confirms what we already believe— that better players win more often, that stronger software produces better outcomes, that expertise and tools combine in predictable ways.

That is not what the researchers found.

The team from MIT and Sun Yat-sen University had set out to study human-AI collaboration in competitive settings. Chess offered a clean laboratory: measurable outcomes, documented performance histories, and a long tradition of humans working alongside computer engines. The expectation was straightforward. They would analyze the data, identify the factors that predicted success, and confirm that some combination of human skill and machine capability explained the results.

Instead, they found an anomaly.

Buried within those figures was a pattern that refused to fit existing models. The best performers were not necessarily the strongest players. They were not using superior software. Some highly skilled players (grandmasters, even!) performed worse when paired with AI than less credentialed competitors. Some players using modest software outperformed others with access to far more powerful engines.

Something was happening in the space between player and program, something that could not be explained by either human skill or machine capability alone.

> **KEY INSIGHT:** *Quality Over Capability.*
> The quality of human-AI collaboration mattered more than raw capability on either side.

In June 2005, the website playchess.com hosted a "freestyle" chess tournament with substantial prize money. Teams could consist of any combination of humans and computers. Several grandmasters entered, working with powerful chess engines. The winner? Not a grandmaster with a supercomputer. Two amateur players from New Hampshire: Steven Cramton (rated 1685) and Zackary Stephen (rated 1381), using three ordinary computers.

This is how scientific discoveries often begin. Not with a dramatic breakthrough, but with a nagging inconsistency. A result that should not exist. A pattern that refuses to dissolve under scrutiny.

The researchers tested alternative explanations. Perhaps the anomaly reflected experience with computers generally—technical proficiency, comfort with interfaces, familiarity with the specific software being used? They had controlled for computer literacy and the pattern persisted. Perhaps it reflected some unmeasured aspect of chess skill, a strategic flexibility that showed up in collaboration but not in standard ratings? They had controlled for that too. The pattern held.

What emerged from the analysis was something unexpected: the existence of a distinct capability, separate from human intelligence, separate from technical skill, separate from the power of the AI itself. A capability that predicted performance in human-AI collaboration independently of all the factors that were supposed to matter.

They called it Artificial Intelligence Quotient. AIQ.

I have spent my career studying patterns—in celestial movements, in human behavior, in the spaces where randomness reveals underlying order. When I first encountered this research, I recognized what they had found. Why? Because the shape of discovery is familiar. The research had the quality of something that had always been there, waiting to be named.

The researchers had identified a new human capability that was already operating, invisibly, whenever humans worked with intelligent systems.

Some professionals demonstrated it in abundance. Others did not. And until this study, no one had thought to measure it, because no one had realized there was something to measure.

The research design itself demonstrates methodological sophistication that establishes AIQ's validity as a genuine capability.

The study took place in three waves:

Wave 1: Established baseline measures controlling for IQ, social intelligence, computer literacy, AI literacy, and demographics.

Wave 2: Occurring just one day later, extracted a single AIQ factor from four distinct ChatGPT tasks: brainstorming, Remote Associates Test (RAT), intellective reasoning, and arithmetic decisions. This single factor explained performance variance across all tasks.

Wave 3: The critical validation arrived. Conducted three weeks after Wave 2, participants performed tasks using an entirely different AI platform, *Renju game AI*.

The AIQ factor measured with ChatGPT predicted success with this completely different system ($\beta = 0.18$, $p < 0.001$). This cross-platform, cross-time prediction demonstrates that AIQ measures a stable, general capability rather than platform-specific knowledge or task-specific skill.

Concurrent validity was confirmed through grammar correction tasks using ChatGPT ($\beta = 0.32$, $p < 0.001$). Extended validation using Gemini tasks in a separate study with UK/US samples found the pattern held across a third platform, longer timeframe, and different cultural contexts ($\beta = 0.20$, $p < 0.001$).

This is what distinguishes genuine intelligence constructs from superficial skills: stability across contexts, platforms, and time. AIQ is not *"being good with ChatGPT."* It is a fundamental capability that transfers.

Another aspect to consider is the strange thing about intelligence. We assume we know what it is and that we can recognize it. And then, every few decades, we discover that we were missing an entire dimension.

Here is something interesting that transpired in Paris in 1904:

The French Ministry of Education faced a problem. The *Jules Ferry* laws of 1882 had mandated universal schooling, which meant classrooms now included children with vastly different learning needs. Teachers struggled. Some students couldn't follow basic instruction while others raced ahead. The ministry needed a way to identify which children required additional support but they wanted something more objective than a teacher's intuition or a doctor's impression.

They turned to Alfred Binet, a self-taught psychologist who had spent fifteen years studying how children think. Binet was an unusual choice. He had no doctoral degree, no formal teaching position. He had built his career outside the establishment, conducting meticulous observations of his own two daughters, developing experimental methods that prioritized evidence over theory. But he had a reputation for rigor, and more importantly, he had an idea.

Alfred Binet Jr. (1857–1911). The glasses observe. The mustache concludes.

Working with his colleague Théodore Simon, Binet assembled a series of tasks, thirty in all, arranged from simple to complex. Could the child follow a moving object with their eyes? Name familiar items in pictures? Repeat a string of numbers? Complete a sentence? The tasks themselves were not the innovation. The breakthrough was Binet's realization that what mattered was the age at which children could complete them. A seven-year-old who performed like a typical five-year-old was behind. One who performed like a typical nine-year-old was ahead. Intelligence, Binet proposed, could be understood as "mental age" relative to chronological age.

The *Binet-Simon Scale*, published in 1905 and revised in 1908, became the foundation of modern intelligence testing. But Binet was careful about what he had created. He insisted that his test measured a narrow slice of mental ability, not some fixed essence of intelligence. *"The scale, properly speaking, does not permit the measure of intelligence,"* he wrote, "because intellectual qualities are not superposable, and therefore cannot be measured as linear surfaces are measured." He worried that his invention would be misused and that a single score would be treated as a permanent judgment rather than a practical tool for helping children learn.

His fears proved prescient. When the test crossed the Atlantic, American psychologists like Lewis Terman and H.H. Goddard stripped away Binet's caveats. Terman's 1916 Stanford-Binet test introduced the *"Intelligence Quotient"*, a single number that Binet never endorsed. Within a decade, IQ testing had become an industry, used not just to help struggling students but to sort, rank, and sometimes exclude professionals based on a number that its inventor never believed could capture the full complexity of the human mind.

The controversy was fierce. Critics argued the tests were culturally biased, that they measured schooling rather than innate ability, that reducing intelligence to a number was reductive and potentially dangerous. And yet, despite all the legitimate concerns, IQ tests turned out to measure something. Something that predicted academic performance, job success, and life outcomes in ways that could not be entirely explained away. The debate continues today, but no serious researcher denies that cognitive ability exists and varies between professionals.

Alfred Binet published his intelligence scale in 1905, but he warned against treating scores as fixed or defining: *"Some recent thinkers have affirmed that an individual's intelligence is a fixed quantity, a quantity that cannot be increased,"* he wrote. *"We must protest and react against this brutal pessimism."*

Despite his caution, IQ became one of psychology's most influential and controversial concepts, eventually predicting outcomes from academic achievement to occupational success across hundreds of studies spanning a century.

In the spring of 1990, as Depeche Mode's "Policy of Truth" began to dominate the airwaves, insisting that *"never again is what you swore the time before"* and the United States watched the Soviet Union slowly exhale its last breaths of the Cold War, two psychologists were preparing a *glasnost* of their own.

Peter Salovey of Yale and John Mayer of the University of New Hampshire published a paper in the journal *Imagination, Cognition and Personality* that functioned as a sort of intellectual arson. They were treading on heretical ground. For much of the twentieth century, the psychological establishment viewed emotion as static on the radio, the noise that ruined the signal. Their own policy of truth was a radical one: they argued that feelings weren't just something to be managed or repressed, but were a rigorous source of information.

The mid-century consensus had been clinical and unforgiving. In his 1943 text *Emotion in Man and Animal*, Paul Young defined emotion as a *"disorganized response which proceeds from a lack of effective adjustment."* To the behaviorists of the time, pure emotion was a *"complete loss of cerebral control."*

In this sterile intellectual climate, suggesting that a feeling could be a form of intelligence was like suggesting that a storm could be a form of architecture. To the men in lab coats, an emotional outburst was not data; it was a structural failure.

The quiet academic ripple became a cultural tsunami in 1995 when science journalist Daniel Goleman published *Emotional Intelligence*. Goleman did not just summarize Salovey and Mayer; he supercharged them. He claimed "EQ" was the secret sauce of life success, the reason the "B" student ends up owning the company while the "A" student calculates the payroll.

Suddenly, "EQ" was everywhere, appearing in Harvard Business Review articles and on the back of cereal boxes. As the public swooned, the ivory tower grew defensive. The academic community, sensing their rigorous construct was being diluted into a participation trophy for the sensitive, launched a counter-offensive.

In 1998, Michèle Davies, Lazar Stankov, and Richard D. Roberts published a pointed critique in the *Journal of Personality and Social Psychology* titled "Emotional Intelligence: In Search of an Elusive Construct." Their conclusion was the academic equivalent of a cold shower: the data simply did not exist.

By 2002, Roberts had doubled down with *Science and Myth* (MIT Press), a 700-page doorstop designed to crush the EQ craze under the weight of empirical doubt. The sharpest tongue belonged to Edwin Locke. In 2005, writing for the *Journal of Organizational Behavior*, Locke argued that "EI" was a linguistic sleight of hand. He claimed it was merely IQ applied to a specific topic or just happiness wearing a lab coat. To Locke, the idea that EI predicted success was less a scientific fact and more a hopeful bedtime story.

Salovey and Mayer, however, were not merely feeling their way through the dark. They spent the early 2000s perfecting the Mayer-Salovey-Caruso Emotional Intelligence Test (MSCEIT). Unlike the popular self-report quizzes, which essentially asked *"Are you a nice person?"* the MSCEIT was an ability test. It asked subjects to identify the specific micro-expressions on a face or predict how a person's mood would shift if their life circumstances were upended.

The persistence worked. The skeptics did not just go away; they were co-opted. David Caruso later noted with a dry smirk that by 2004, Richard D. Roberts—the man who had spent a decade calling EI a myth—was busy organizing a scientific symposium to define its taxonomy. The skeptics had been invited to the faculty lounge, finally forced to admit that the messy business of human feeling might just be the most sophisticated software we own.

In the professional world, corporate executives who had risen through the ranks on analytical ability alone discovered that their most effective leaders were often those who could read a room, navigate conflict, and inspire teams. Organizations including *Johnson & Johnson* funded studies examining the relationship between emotional intelligence and leadership performance. The research accumulated: EQ predicted leadership effectiveness, team performance, resilience

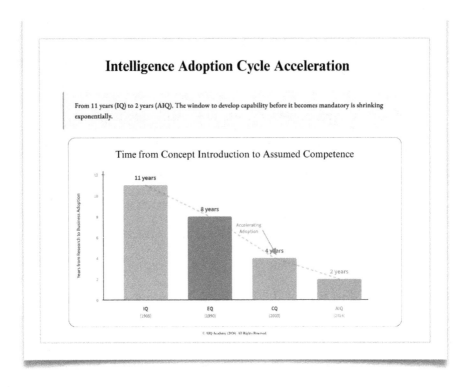

Intelligence Adoption Cycle Acceleration

From 11 years (IQ) to 2 years (AIQ). The window to develop capability before it becomes mandatory is shrinking exponentially.

Time from Concept Introduction to Assumed Competence

under pressure, and relationship quality in ways that IQ alone could not.

What had been dismissed as *"soft skills"* became strategically essential. Today, emotional intelligence training is a multi-billion dollar industry, and few serious discussions of leadership development omit it.

The temporal compression is exponential and empirically measurable.

IQ (1905–1916): 11 years from Alfred Binet's introduction of mental testing to Lewis Terman's Stanford-Binet standardization and widespread adoption in military selection, educational placement, and occupational screening.

EQ (1990–1998): 8 years from Salovey and Mayer's academic introduction to Johnson & Johnson's commissioned study demonstrating business impact and corporate adoption of emotional intelligence frameworks.

CQ (2003–2007): 4 years from Earley and Ang's framework establishment to validated measurement instruments and integration into global leadership development programs.

AIQ (2024–2026+): Approximately 2 years from MIT/Sun Yat-sen publication to assessment availability and enterprise implementation.

This acceleration is not arbitrary. Each intelligence form faced initial skepticism, then rigorous validation, then business adoption. But the cycle compresses with each iteration. IQ required a world war to prove its utility. EQ required bestselling books and decades of leadership research. CQ benefited from globalization urgency. AIQ arrives when AI has already penetrated knowledge work, when organizations face immediate performance divergence, when waiting for academic consensus is economically untenable.

The window for voluntary development before AIQ becomes table stakes is not decades. It is months. This is the documented acceleration of intelligence adoption cycles over 120 years.

AIQ belongs in this lineage.

KEY INSIGHT: *Kasparov's Process Principle.*
Garry Kasparov, writing in *The New York Review of Books* (February 2010) about the 2005 freestyle tournament results, articulated what has become known as *Kasparov's Law*: *"Weak human + machine + better process was superior to a strong computer alone and, more remarkably, superior to a strong human + machine + inferior process."*

The quality of the collaboration process, how you work with AI, matters more than raw capability on either side. This insight, drawn from competitive chess, anticipated what the researchers would later demonstrate with rigorous longitudinal data.

The research, led by Xin Qin at Sun Yat-sen University and Jackson Lu at MIT Sloan School of Management, was published in late 2024. By then, artificial intelligence had already become embedded in knowledge work across industries. Millions of professionals were collaborating with AI systems daily, writing, analyzing and deciding with them. The capability that the researchers identified was not a future concern. It was already determining outcomes, creating divergence and separating professionals who produced extraordinary results from professionals who struggled with the same tools.

Yet almost no one knew the AIQ research existed.

Why didn't this study make headlines? Why wasn't it on the cover of every business magazine?

Because we are saturated with AI spectacle. Headlines compete for attention with predictions of utopia or catastrophe. Jobs will be eliminated or transformed. Creativity democratized or destroyed. Humanity augmented or replaced. The noise is so loud, constant, and emotionally charged that quieter findings struggled to penetrate.

A careful, longitudinal study about human-AI collaboration had little chance of breaking through. It lacked drama and offered no apocalypse and no miracle cure. It asked readers to sit with nuance at a moment when the public conversation rewarded certainty and speed. The researchers published in academic journals, presented at conferences, accumulated citations from fellow scholars—but the finding that could transform how millions of professionals approach their work remained buried in the technical literature.

Until now.

What the research showed was not that AI would replace human intelligence. Nor that human intelligence would remain supreme. It showed something more interesting and more consequential: that a new form of intelligence emerges in the collaboration itself. Not human. Not machine. Something that exists only in the interaction between the two.

And this new intelligence—this AIQ—varies dramatically from person to person. Consider three professionals in the same role at the same company, using the same AI tools.

The **first** produces work that astonishes. Her strategic memos synthesize market dynamics that no one else had connected. Her presentations anticipate objections before they're raised. Her analysis reveals patterns that inform decisions worth millions. Colleagues wonder how she does it, whether she has some special access, some secret prompt, some technical advantage no one else has discovered. She doesn't. She has the same tools everyone else has. She simply uses them differently.

The **second** produces competent work. His reports are accurate. His analysis is solid. The AI makes him faster, maybe more efficient, but not fundamentally better. His output is professional and unremarkable. The ceiling on what he produces remains roughly where it was before AI arrived. He works hard, prompts carefully, generates outputs that meet expectations without exceeding them.

The **third** performs worse with AI than he did without it. His drafts now require more editing than when he wrote from scratch. His analysis contains subtle errors he doesn't catch, plausible-sounding conclusions that don't hold up under scrutiny. He spends more time managing the AI than he would have spent doing the work directly. The assistance has become friction. He's not sure why, but working with AI feels harder than it should.

These three professionals exist in every organization, industry and country where AI tools have become available. The patterns the researchers documented in chess tournaments, where some players thrived in collaboration with AI while others floundered, replicate everywhere humans work alongside intelligent systems.

KEY INSIGHT: *AIQ Is Distinct from Traditional Intelligence.*
Those with high intelligence did not automatically demonstrate high AIQ. Technically skilled users did not reliably outperform others. The capability being measured is genuinely new. It exists only in the interaction between human and machine, and it varies independently of other measures of competence.

The gap between these groups is widening.

Not slowly, over decades, in ways that professionals can gradually adapt to but quickly and measurably. In ways that are already reshaping who gets hired, who gets promoted, who produces valuable work and who does not.

This is not a prediction about the future. This is documentation of what is already happening. And most professionals are navigating this shift without knowing that AIQ exists, let alone where they stand relative to others.

AIQ 2026 will change that. This book will teach you what AIQ is, how it operates, and why it matters. It will show you the five dimensions that comprise AIQ, dimensions that you can observe, understand, and develop. It will give you concrete examples of what high AIQ looks like in practice, drawn from historical figures who mastered these capabilities before they had names.

And then it will ask you to do something that most books do not ask: to measure your own AIQ to reveal where you truly stand, not where you hope you stand.

In 2023, while analyzing patterns in my own work with AI, I began noticing something that didn't fit existing frameworks. Some approaches produced extraordinary results. Others, seemingly similar, produced mediocrity. The difference wasn't my effort, and it wasn't the prompts themselves. Something else was operating, something consistent, something that seemed to transfer across different tasks and tools.

When I encountered the MIT research in early 2024, I recognized what they had found. Their rigorous longitudinal data confirmed what I had been observing. But the research stopped at identification. It proved AIQ existed. It did not provide a way for individuals to measure their own capability or develop what needed developing.

> **KEY INSIGHT:** *AIQ Is Real.*
> AIQ is a genuine capability, not a fleeting skill or temporary advantage. Like IQ or EQ, it reflects something fundamental about how you think and work.

In the chapters that follow, I will demonstrate highly refined AIQ patterns through five remarkable historical figures—Cleopatra, Kahlil Gibran, David Hume, Sen no Rikyū, and Lise Meitner—each of whom mastered one of the five dimensions before AI existed. I will share frameworks for observing yourself more carefully and recognizing the difference between collaboration and tool usage.

The guarantees are gone. The patterns are visible. The divergence has already begun. What remains is the question: what do you do now that you know AIQ is real? Let's begin.

Chapter 2: The Guarantees Are Gone

B y 2030, 92 million jobs will be displaced globally while 170 million new ones are created. That is a net gain of 78 million positions. 59% of workers will require re-skilling or up-skilling by 2030, and 120 million workers are at medium-term risk of redundancy.

You are already seeing this shift. Business does not behave like it used to. Traditional career paths are disappearing. The guarantees that once protected knowledge workers, things like credentials, experience, institutional affiliation, no longer hold.

AI could affect approximately 300 million full-time equivalent jobs globally, with its impact expected to be most disruptive in the next 10 - 30 years.

But the real story is not about AI *"taking"* jobs. It's about AI revealing a capability gap that's been invisible, until now.

For most of the twentieth century, the answer to *"how do I support myself?"* would have sounded obvious. You acquired knowledge, demonstrated competence and exchanged your time for financial stability. The transaction was clear, even if no one wrote it down. You studied, you credentialed, you proved yourself—and in return, institutions gave you work, structure, audience, and if you were fortunate, benefits. A pension. Health insurance. The quiet assurance that loyalty would be rewarded with continuity.

This was not a universal experience. It was never available to everyone equally. But it was the dominant model, the assumed trajectory, the thing that shaped how parents advised children and how young professionals planned their lives. Get the degree. Get the job. Stay long enough. The system will take care of you.

'Choose life. Choose a job. Choose a career. Choose a family. Choose a big television. Choose washing machines, cars, compact disc players, and electrical tin openers. Choose good health, low cholesterol, and dental insurance. Choose fixed-interest mortgage repayments. Choose your friends. Choose leisurewear and matching luggage. Choose DIY and wondering who the f you are on a Sunday morning. Choose sitting on that couch watching mind-numbing spirit-crushing game shows, stuffing junk food into your mouth. Choose rotting away at the end of it all. But why would I want to do a thing like that?'

— *Irvine Welsh, Trainspotting (1996)*

What has changed is not the value of intelligence. Intelligence still matters—perhaps more than ever. What has changed is who is responsible for converting that intelligence into livelihood.

Increasingly, that responsibility sits with you.

I want to be careful here, because this shift is easy to misread. It is not that institutions have vanished. Companies still exist. Universities still grant degrees. Professional associations still certify competence. The infrastructure of the old system remains standing.

What has thinned is the promise underneath. The promise was never explicit. No one handed you a contract that said: *"In exchange for your time, loyalty and competence, we guarantee you a career."* But the promise operated anyway, embedded in expectations, reinforced by decades of precedent. Professionals who did the right things—who followed the path, who accumulated the credentials, who showed up and performed—could reasonably expect the system to absorb them. To find a place for them. To convert their time and effort into security.

That conversion no longer happens automatically.

The evidence is everywhere, for those willing to see it. In 2025 alone, nearly 55,000 job cuts in the United States were directly attributed to artificial intelligence, according to the outplacement firm Challenger, Gray & Christmas, out of a total 1.17 million layoffs, the highest since the pandemic year of 2020. Since 2023, more than 71,000 jobs have been explicitly linked to AI displacement.

Amazon eliminated 14,000 corporate roles, with CEO Andy Jassy stating directly that AI enables *"leaner structures."* Microsoft cut 15,000 positions. Salesforce reduced its customer support workforce by 4,000, with CEO Marc Benioff acknowledging that AI now handles roughly half the company's support volume. These are not rumors or projections. The shrinking of the labor force is no longer a matter of backroom rumor or quiet projection. It is, instead, a point of corporate pride, shouted from the rooftops of press releases and whispered, with a certain manic glee, into the ears of shareholders during earnings calls. Executives are no longer hiding the knife; they are explaining, with unsettling clarity, exactly why fewer humans will be needed to keep the gears turning.

KEY INSIGHT: *The Language of Layoffs Has Changed.*
What companies once called *"restructuring"* is now openly called *"automation."* The honesty is new. The displacement is not.

This shift creates a fragmented, hallucinatory experience for the job seeker. You see roles posted for positions that never seem to be filled, *"ghost jobs"* used to project growth that isn't there. You find listings that demand the expertise of a senior executive but offer the wages of an intern. On platforms like LinkedIn and Indeed, the reality of the market does not align with the optimism of the interface. You watch roles vanish and realize they aren't coming back; they have been absorbed into software or redistributed across the remaining, overworked staff. You have done everything right but find yourself outside the flow of opportunity, watching a labor market that no longer seems to recognize you.

This is a story about risk, where it sits, and who absorbs it.

For decades, institutions absorbed risk on behalf of individuals. Consider how IBM operated from the 1950s through the 1980s: the company famously maintained a *"full employment"* policy, retaining workers through economic downturns and retraining them for new roles rather than cutting headcount. When mainframe sales declined, IBM invested in moving employees into services and software. The implicit message was clear: if you gave the company your loyalty, the company would protect your livelihood.

That era ended within living memory. And its end was deliberate.

Now institutions optimize continuously. A *Harvard Business Review* analysis of layoff practices describes the modern approach bluntly: companies have shifted from episodic restructuring during genuine crises to *"routine layoffs"* as a standard management tool. The research shows that these cuts rarely achieve their stated financial goals—the short-term savings are typically overshadowed by lost institutional knowledge, weakened employee engagement, higher voluntary turnover among survivors, and reduced innovation. Yet the practice accelerates because financial markets reward it. Stock prices often rise on layoff announcements, regardless of whether the cuts make operational sense.

They shed cost when cost becomes inconvenient. They speak of agility and flexibility, which are real virtues for organizations, and real risks for those inside them. The individual is no longer buffered by the institution. Now, the individual is exposed.

KEY INSIGHT: *Risk Has Been Transferred.*

For decades, institutions absorbed economic uncertainty on behalf of employees. Now individuals absorb it on behalf of institutions.

I recently spoke with a friend over drinks in Baja Norte, Mexico. She is a senior executive in human resources with over twenty years of experience in talent management, spanning both the manufacturing and financial services sectors. She is a thoughtful, candid person who has spent her career observing the inner workings of large organizations.

And during our conversation she shared an observation that has stayed with me.

She explained that once employees reach a certain age, typically around fifty, it becomes increasingly difficult to justify their presence on a corporate balance sheet. This has nothing to do with their output. In many cases, these individuals are among the highest performers in the company. They are the ones with the most institutional knowledge, having successfully navigated decades of technological shifts and corporate restructuring.

The issue is purely financial.

As employees age, the cost of their health benefits increases. Their salaries, which have grown through years of tenure and experience, are significantly higher than those of newer entrants. From a strictly mathematical perspective, the system now favors replacing a veteran worker with a younger hire. Even if the younger employee lacks experience and requires extensive training, and even if they make mistakes a veteran would avoid, the lower salary and benefit costs often make the replacement look like a gain on paper.

She didn't describe this as a personal failing of leadership, but as a matter of systemic efficiency. It is simply the way the math is done now.

I think about that often. It is a sobering reality for those who followed the rules, adapted to every change, and survived every previous disruption, only to find that the experience they worked so hard to gain is now viewed as a financial liability.

The data bears this out. A landmark 2014 U.S. Bureau of Labor Statistics analysis found that workers aged fifty-five and older who lose a job experience significantly longer periods of unemployment than their younger counterparts. Recent 2025 analyses show that roughly 32 percent of job seekers in this age bracket are classified as long-term unemployed—searching for more than six months—compared with 24.5 percent of younger workers.

And once re-employed, these veterans are far more likely to accept a significant pay cut or simply exit the workforce entirely. The experience they spent decades accumulating is often treated as a sunk cost rather than a value add. For those who do manage to pivot into new industries, the transition frequently comes with an earnings penalty of up to 30 percent, a financial reset that effectively erases years of hard-won progress.

In the modern market, experience has become a paradoxical currency: the more you have, the less the system seems willing to pay for it.

> **KEY INSIGHT:** *Experience x Friction.*
>
> Experience, once treated as the ultimate protection, now functions as friction. The very tenure that should signal value has become a cost to be optimized away.

This shift makes me uncomfortable. More than uncomfortable. It has knocked me sideways in ways that I am still processing.

I was raised with the same assumptions you likely were. Work hard. Get credentials. Prove yourself. The system will recognize you. The system will find a place for you. I believed this because everyone around me believed it, and because for a long time, it seemed true.

So, I followed the rules. All of them.

I raised four children. I went back to school part-time, starting at Santa Monica community college as a single mother. It was a humbling experience, sitting in fluorescent-lit classrooms with eighteen-year-olds while selecting classes based on my children's school schedule. For twenty years, nearly all of my free time was devoted to two things: my children and my education. I missed social gatherings. I let friendships thin. I told myself it would be worth it, that I was building something, that the sacrifice had a payoff waiting at the end.

I graduated *summa cum laude* from Arizona State University. That alone was hard in the unglamorous way: working, studying, starting over more than once, and learning how to keep going when momentum disappears.

After that, I did something that still feels slightly improbable. I was admitted to Harvard University and completed my master's degree, graduating with the Class of 2020. My two year degree took six years, not because of academic weakness, but because of life logistics and values.

For six years, I commuted back and forth to Cambridge. I chose every class based on what would allow me to never miss time with my children. My academic path was dictated less by intellectual curiosity than by visit schedules and school calendars. I selected courses that met on the weekends I didn't have my children. If those weekends had fallen differently, I likely wouldn't be an international relations graduate at all. My degree exists because of scheduling math as much as academic ambition.

Early in the program, I took a course on game theoretical models of conflict. I grew up in Los Angeles, so when the professor started talking about *models*, I briefly assumed—incorrectly—that this meant models in the runway sense. Or possibly actors. As in film actors. When the syllabus kept referring to *"actors behaving rationally,"* I wondered why anyone thought actors were rational at all. Brad Pitt, again, was not part of the curriculum. It took me longer than I care to admit to realize that *modeling conflict* does not involve attractive professionals or dramatic monologues. It involves math. And abstractions. And assumptions about human behavior that are deeply uncomfortable once you realize how fragile they are.

For the entire six years, I had the persistent sensation that I was the least intelligent person in the room. That feeling did not go away with time, grades, or familiarity. Even in my final class, with graduation in sight, I was convinced everyone else understood something fundamental that I had somehow missed.

What I understand now, after Harvard, Yale and MIT is this:

Real learning is uncomfortable.

Many professionals spend their lives trying to avoid that sensation. They want fluency without friction, mastery without disorientation, answers without having to sit in the not-knowing. When things feel confusing or destabilizing, they assume something has gone wrong. But that discomfort is the signal.

Each system we were raised to trust, education, work, expertise, and authority, are all changing at once. There is no way to understand that shift without feeling unsettled. Anyone who claims this transition is painless is either selling something or hasn't looked closely enough.

You can finish the degree. You can do the work. You can raise children and sit in University classrooms where you feel completely unqualified. And that feeling may stay with you. That doesn't mean you're failing. It means you're learning. And, yes, I graduated Class of 2020. The only graduating class since Harvard's founding in 1636 without an in-person commencement ceremony.

I was never able to see my name pop up on the Zoom. My diploma arrived by mail, in a cardboard tube, while I sat in sweats wondering if the mailman understood the significance of what he had just handed me. Nearly four centuries of graduates walked through Harvard Yard, and my class got a webinar and a FedEx tracking number.

Come to think of it, I also got my real estate license in 2007, right before the housing market collapsed. I am starting to suspect there is a small black cloud that follows my career milestones around, checking its calendar.

I continued to MIT and Yale for executive education. I did everything the path demanded. I sacrificed more than I can easily describe. And then I came out the other side and discovered that the whole job market had shifted while I was in the library.

Position after position, I applied. Eventually, I would learn that they decided to hire from within. Credentials that should have opened doors led only to polite rejections. After twenty years of doing everything right—following every instruction, accumulating every credential, making every sacrifice—I found myself standing outside the very structures I had worked so hard to enter. The system that was supposed to recognize me did not seem to know I existed.

There is a specific kind of emotional labor involved in the job search that rarely gets discussed. To apply for a role is not merely to send a PDF into a vacuum; it is an act of imagination. In plain English, you have to picture yourself getting the job and working at the place. After my third round of interviews for an incredible position, I found myself doing dry runs of the commute, timing the distance between my front door and my new, hypothetical office. I researched local schools and sat with my spouse over a shared charcuterie board to map out the logistics of a move, calculating whether the opportunity was worth the disruption to our children's lives. We were giddy. It felt as though all the years of sacrifice were finally coalescing into a new chapter.

I even began the work of physical transformation. I reviewed the contents of my closet and realized, with a sinking clarity, that my wardrobe—a collection of stay-at-home mom practicalities and student staples—would never survive the "muckety-muck" world of this new position. I was already mentally clearing out the old self to make room for the new one.

But I didn't get the job.

And it wasn't just that one. It was again, and again, and again. For three years, I lived in this cycle of searching, planning, and performing. For one position, I wrote pages of dense, thoughtful answers to essay-like questions, pouring my intellectual capital into a portal that offered nothing back. Each time, the sting was the same.

A job search is a family's collective breath, held in anticipation. But there is a profound cruelty in the imbalance of weight. While you are measuring the future of your family and auditing your closet for a new identity, the company on the other end often fails to give you any weight at all. You have mentally rearranged your entire world for them, but to the institution, you are a data point that hasn't yet been "optimized."

It has been incredibly difficult to reconcile that silence. Yet, the hardest part was not the rejection itself; it was the realization of what I would have to do instead.

The research was clear. The path forward was not more credentials, more applications, more waiting for institutions to notice me. The path forward was visibility. Building my own audience. Becoming front-facing. Taking responsibility for making my own work known rather than trusting others to discover it.

For someone like me, this felt almost impossible.

I am a very private person. I spent twenty years at home with my family, and commuting to University. I am not used to putting myself out there. The thought of self-promotion, of making myself visible, of building a *"personal brand"* felt uncomfortable in a way I struggled to articulate. It felt undignified. It felt like admitting defeat.

After decades of contribution, after proving yourself again and again within established structures, the suggestion that you must now promote yourself can feel almost insulting. Self-promotion was for those who hadn't earned their place. For individuals without *"real"* credentials. For influencers and hustlers, not those of us who had spent years doing serious work in quiet rooms.

I understand this resistance because I have lived the full weight of not wanting to *be* that person, the one self-promoting, building a brand, making herself visible. Of wanting the work to speak for itself. Of believing, despite all evidence, that if I just kept my head down and did good work, someone would eventually notice.

But here is what I have learned, and it has been humbling to learn it: the resistance is not protecting you. It is keeping you attached to a system that is no longer holding up its end of the bargain.

I had to get over being private. Not because I wanted to, but because the alternative was invisibility.

> **KEY INSIGHT:** *qui non videtur, perit.*
>
> *"He who is not seen, perishes."* Invisibility in 2026+ is a slow kind of professional death.

I had to learn to do things that felt deeply uncomfortable and accept that the rules I had followed for twenty years were no longer the rules in effect. I had to be willing to build something new, from scratch, at an age when I had expected to be coasting on accumulated credibility.

It's hard to consider and it's even harder to do. And I want you to know that if you are feeling any of this, the discomfort, the resistance, the sense that something unfair has happened, you are not alone. I have felt all of it. I am still feeling it.

The shift I am describing is not about age, although age makes it more visible. It affects our youth too, in different ways. They enter a labor market that offers credentials without clear paths, opportunities without stability, flexibility that is really just precarity by another name.

But the shift hits differently depending on where you are in your career.

If you are early, you have time to adapt. You can build new skills, establish visibility, create optionality before the pressure becomes acute. The discomfort is real but the runway is long.

If you are mid-career or later, the calculus changes. You may have obligations—mortgage, children, aging parents—that constrain your choices. You may have spent decades building expertise that the market now values less than it once did. You may have assumed that by this point, the hard part would be over.

And now you discover that the hard part is just beginning. Not because you failed, but because the terrain shifted beneath everyone.

Here is the uncomfortable truth at the center of this chapter.

The skills that protected us before no longer function as protection.

Not because those skills were wrong. They were right for their time. Holding information mattered when information was scarce. Credentials mattered when credentials were reliable signals. Institutional affiliation mattered when institutions absorbed risk and distributed opportunity.

Those skills fail now not because education failed, but because scarcity did.

Information is no longer scarce. Anyone can access almost anything instantly. The advantage no longer goes to those who possess knowledge; it goes to individuals who can synthesize, contextualize and apply under conditions of uncertainty.

Credentials are no longer reliable signals. And to be honest, too many professionals have them. Too many paths exist outside them. The market has learned that a degree predicts less than it used to, and pedigree predicts less than performance.

Institutional affiliation no longer guarantees anything. You can do everything right inside an organization and still find yourself outside it, for reasons that have nothing to do with your contribution and everything to do with a spreadsheet you will never see.

This is a more challenging problem which requires different skills. And it requires a willingness to take responsibility for things that used to be handled by others.

I am sharing this because I believe that clarity, even uncomfortable clarity, is better than comfortable illusion. Those who navigate this shift successfully will be the ones who see it clearly. Who understands that the rules have changed. Who stops waiting for the old system to reassert itself and start building for the system that actually exists.

I understood this more clearly after a call I was invited to join with Mustafa Suleyman, the CEO of Microsoft AI. Before that call, I had never heard of him—my limited experience with Microsoft products meant I was not tracking its leadership. Then Allie K. Miller introduced him as someone akin to *the Beyoncé of AI,* and suddenly I was paying very close attention.

The comparison was not hyperbole.

What followed exceeded every expectation. Suleyman spoke about artificial intelligence the way a poet speaks about language—with precision and wonder simultaneously. He talked about emotional intelligence in AI systems, about the texture of how humans and machines might work together rather than simply coexist. At one point, he said something that has stayed with me: "I focus more on the EQ of the models."

Without using the term, he was describing the essence of AIQ.

KEY INSIGHT: *Recognize the Distinction.*

"I focus more on the EQ of the models." — Mustafa Suleyman, CEO of Microsoft AI.

The most profound breakthroughs come from understanding the distinctly human capacities that give the machine direction.

It was one of those rare moments when the universe seems to align, when you jump on a call with no expectations and emerge with knowledge that reshapes your understanding of what is possible. Suleyman articulated something I had been circling for years: that the most profound breakthroughs come not from mastering the machine, but from understanding the distinctly human capacities that give the machine direction. The tools are everywhere now. The capability to use them well, to bring emotional intelligence, contextual judgment, creative vision to the collaboration, that remains rare.

I will tell you something I have not told many. While I was on that call, listening to Suleyman describe what he was building, all I wanted to do was reach out to him. To tell him about the research I had discovered. About AIQ. About what I had been working on. The connection between what he was saying and what I had found felt so immediate, so alive.

And I did not do it.

I meant to. I told myself I would. But then I thought: what am I thinking? That I can reach out to someone that accomplished, that important? Who am I to contact his office? I was just glad to be on the call. So I stayed quiet. I let the moment pass. I was nervous, and the nervousness won.

I think about that a lot now.

One of my goals for 2026 is to reach out to his team with this book. I have learned something important about this new landscape: you can try. That is one thing that has changed. With LinkedIn, email, DM's and all the tools we have now, you can get in touch with just about anyone. Most professionals don't, because they talk themselves out of it (the way I did after that call).

The good news is that what sets you apart is not access. Access is more available than ever. What sets you apart is the knowledge and the preparation you bring. The willingness to try when everything in you says you are not important enough, not credentialed enough, not connected enough.

KEY INSIGHT: *Access is no longer the barrier.*

With DM's, LinkedIn and email, you can reach almost anyone. What sets you apart is the knowledge and preparation you bring—and the willingness to try when everything in you says you are not enough.

You can try. I want to encourage you to try. The worst that happens is silence. The best that happens might change everything.

This is where intelligence reasserts itself. Not as credential, not as accumulated knowledge, not as proof of having passed through the right gates. Intelligence as synthesis. Intelligence as creation. Intelligence as the capacity to make sense of complexity and offer something valuable to others.

The question is no longer: what do you know? The question is: what can you create from what you know that others will value? And how will they find out about it?

This is the new landscape. The guarantees are gone. The institutions that once carried you will not carry you anymore. What remains is your ability to think, to create, to make yourself useful in ways that are visible to those who matter.

And this is exactly where AIQ becomes decisive.

The capacity to collaborate effectively with AI, to produce high-quality work in partnership with intelligent systems, is now one of the primary ways that intelligence converts to value. It is not the only way. But it is an increasingly central one.

In the next chapter, I will show you what this looks like in practice. Two earnest individuals, facing the same circumstances who made different choices and arrived at radically different outcomes.

The difference between them is not luck nor is it traditional intelligence. It is not credentials or connections or any of the things we were all taught to accumulate. The difference is something else, something that can be seen, measured, and developed.

But first, you have to understand what it looks like when it's present, and what it looks like when it is not.

Chapter 3: Two Professionals, Same Storm

Here is how the divide appears in practice:

Sarah M. Portland

Sarah M. turned forty-five in March, just as her employer—a mid-sized healthcare analytics firm—announced its second *"strategic review"* in eighteen months. She'd seen this before. Private equity had acquired a majority stake last year, and now the language in company-wide emails had shifted from *"growth"* to *"optimization."*

Sarah held a director-level role in client services, managing a team of twelve. She'd built her career methodically. She began with an undergraduate degree from Oregon State, MBA from Portland State completed part-time while raising two children, fifteen years with the same company watching it grow from forty employees to nearly three hundred. Her mortgage payment was $3,400 a month. Her daughter was starting at Lewis & Clark in the fall; her son would follow in two years. Her father, recently diagnosed with Parkinson's, was selling the family home in Eugene and would need help navigating that transition.

The margin for error had become very thin.

Her company had policies about AI tools. Officially, they only approved systems. No uploading proprietary information to ChatGPT or Claude would be tolerated. They were reasonable policies, she thought, but they meant whatever AI skills she developed would have to come from her own time, not work time.

When the restructuring rumors started, Sarah did what she had always done. She updated her LinkedIn profile, polished her résumé, highlighting recent wins including the client retention program that had saved three major accounts, and the process improvement initiative that had reduced response times by thirty percent. Sarah reached out to former colleagues, carefully worded messages testing whether anyone had heard of opportunities. She began monitoring Indeed and LinkedIn Jobs, not obsessively, but regularly.

Sarah used AI tools at work within the permitted boundaries. Summarizing meeting notes, drafting client emails and preparing slide decks. It was helpful in small ways, but nothing about how she worked or thought had fundamentally changed.

Outside of her work, she kept telling herself she'd learn AI tools properly once things settled down. Once the restructuring was clarified, her dad's situation stabilized. Mainly she just needed some more time.

There was always a reason to wait.

By June, her father had moved in temporarily while they looked for assisted living options. Someone on her team quit, and the workload redistributed without discussion. Her evenings disappeared into emails and preparation for morning meetings. Weekends became recovery time. The job search continued in fragments—applications sent at 11 PM after everyone else was asleep, networking calls squeezed into lunch breaks.

The responses were sparse. Every director-level position seemed to attract three hundred applicants. The roles that were available paid twenty percent less than what she made now.

Every move she made depended on someone else's decision. Whether to hire her. Whether to keep her. Whether to see her résumé among the hundreds. She was working harder than ever, trying to prove indispensability through sheer effort.

KEY INSIGHT: *Be Willing to Fail*

Passive collaborators don't fear change. Often, they fear being seen trying something new and failing. They repeat what's comfortable, mistaking the absence of failure for the presence of success, until the gap between where they are and where they need to be becomes uncrossable.

Most use AI the way they use a search engine, to ask a question, receive an answer, move on. The interaction is transactional. The human remains passive, a recipient of output rather than a shaper of it. This passive pattern is invisible to the person using it—they feel productive because they're getting outputs, but they're missing the collaboration that creates genuine advantage.

Sarah was behaving exactly as the previous system had trained her to behave: seek validation from institutions, wait for permission, protect reputation, minimize risk.

The problem was that the system no longer rewarded this behavior the way it once did.

Marc F., Chicago

Marc F. also turned forty-five in March. He also worked for a company facing restructuring—a software consultancy where he'd spent thirteen years as a senior solutions architect. He also had financial pressures: mortgage, two teenagers, aging parents in San Francisco whose health was declining.

Like Sarah, Marc faced the same constraints. His employer had similar AI policies. Personal experimentation was discouraged. Whatever adaptation happened would have to occur outside work.

But Marc made a different decision.

He didn't abandon the job search, that would have been reckless, but he decided to split his energy. Half directed at conventional career paths. Half directed at something he'd been curious about for twenty years: traditional watchmaking.

He'd inherited his grandfather's tools when he was thirty, tiny screwdrivers, loupes, a jeweler's workbench that had sat unused in his garage ever since. He'd always meant to learn. He'd taken one weekend workshop in 2008, enjoyed it immensely, then life had intervened. Kids, career, the treadmill of professional middle age.

In late March, Marc set up his grandfather's workbench in the corner of his basement. He ordered a broken vintage Omega Seamaster from eBay for sixty dollars and started documenting the restoration on YouTube.

The first videos were terrible. Poor lighting. Shaky camera work. He spoke too fast, and assumed too much knowledge. But he kept going. Every Sunday morning, he'd work on watches and film what he was learning. This required learning video editing, lighting, sound design, and how to speak naturally to a camera. None of it came easily. But here's where the difference emerged.

Marc used AI not to replace effort but to accelerate learning. When he couldn't figure out why his audio sounded tinny, he didn't just ask Claude *"how do I fix audio?"*

Marc engaged actively: *"I'm recording in a basement with concrete walls. Audio sounds tinny and echoey. I've tried a lapel mic but that didn't help. Here's a sample of what it sounds like. What should I consider?"*

He didn't accept the first answer. He pushed back, tested suggestions, asked follow-up questions that revealed gaps in his own thinking. When Claude suggested acoustic treatment, Marc asked about specific materials, costs, DIY options. When one solution didn't work, he documented why and asked what to try next.

The process was slower than if he'd just accepted whatever AI produced first. But the learning was deeper. His confidence built faster.

> **KEY INSIGHT:** *Active Collaboration vs. Tool Use*
>
> High-AIQ collaboration is conversational, iterative, and demanding. The human is always steering, always evaluating, always refining.

The AI contributes, but the human authors. The result is work that neither could produce alone; a genuine synthesis that emerges from the interaction itself. This is collaboration, not mere tool use.

Professionals started watching. Not many at first, his fifth video got forty-three views, but the audience grew steadily. Watchmakers from Switzerland, Japan, Germany started leaving comments. Questions arrived. A small community formed around those who cared about craft, about authenticity, about things made slowly and carefully.

Marc started writing alongside the videos. Brief reflections in a newsletter about what he was learning. Why mechanical watches mattered in an age of Apple Watches. How traditional craftsmanship differed from industrial manufacturing. The philosophy underneath the practice; precision, patience, the satisfaction of understanding how something works.

Marc used AI to pressure-test his ideas, explore adjacent questions, synthesize what he was learning into frameworks that might resonate.

He wasn't asking AI to write for him. He was thinking with it, challenging its suggestions, refining his own perspective, using the interaction to sharpen rather than shortcut.

When viewers began asking if he offered instruction, Marc was surprised. But he assembled a focused online workshop: *"Restoring Your First Vintage Watch—A Complete Guide."* Ninety minutes, highly specific, priced at $47.

It sold. Then it sold again. Then twenty-three professionals signed up in a single weekend. A modest income stream began forming, not enough to replace his salary, but enough to matter. Enough to prove something real was happening.

Six Months Later

In September, Sarah received the email she'd been dreading. Her position had been eliminated. The language was gentle, *"difficult decision," "changing business needs," "grateful for your contributions,"* but the outcome was final. Severance: four months. Benefits: ninety days.

She did the math that night at the kitchen table after everyone was asleep. Savings would cover three months, maybe four with serious cutbacks. The job search that had been background noise became the only thing that mattered. Applications that had been casual now became urgent. The market that had seemed difficult now seemed impossible.

The ground that had seemed solid, that she'd stood on for fifteen years, had given way. And there was no net beneath.

Marc was in Glashütte, Germany.

He was attending a weeklong intensive at the German School of Watchmaking. It was something he'd wanted to do since his twenties but never thought possible. He'd applied for a scholarship the school offered to digital educators and, to his surprise, won it. The school had been watching his videos. They liked his teaching approach.

While he was learning from master watchmakers, income continued arriving. Course sales. New newsletter subscribers at $7/month. YouTube ad revenue. Patreon supporters. Small streams, but steady, none depending on any single employer or institution.

During the program, he was approached by a small Swiss parts supplier. They'd been watching his content for months. They wanted to sponsor a video series about sourcing authentic vintage parts, a problem many amateur watchmakers struggled with. The terms were favorable: $3,000 for four videos, plus affiliate commissions. The opportunity had emerged not from a job application but from visibility, from having built something others could see and evaluate and trust.

When Marc returned home, he faced the same uncertain economy as Sarah. The same disrupted industries. The same difficult market.

But his experience of that uncertainty was fundamentally different.

Sarah experienced risk as exposure. Every decision that mattered was made by someone else. Whether to hire. Whether to respond. Whether to see her résumé. She was working hard, trying everything, but ultimately waiting for external validation that might never come.

Marc experienced risk as optionality. Multiple income streams, none depending on a single decision-maker. A community that existed independently of any institution. Skills tested in public and validated by professionals willing to pay. He wasn't immune to uncertainty, no one is, but he'd built a structure that absorbed shocks rather than transmitting them directly.

KEY INSIGHT: *The Flood.*

> LinkedIn processes eleven thousand job applications per minute — over fifteen million a day—a 45% increase in a single year. That surge is driven by AI tools auto-generating applications. The system professionals are relying on to find work is being flooded by the same technology that is eliminating their positions. The old path of apply, wait and hope someone sees your résumé is being actively drowned out by automation.
>
> Source: New York Times, June 2025, "The DealBook" Newsletter

What Made the Difference?

The capacity to think clearly *with* your AI tool and to develop ideas iteratively, producing work that exceeds what either humans or machines could create alone. The difference between Sarah and Marc cannot be explained by intelligence in the traditional sense. Both are smart and experienced. Both worked hard, cared about their families, and wanted security.

The difference cannot be explained by luck. The opportunity to experiment was equally available to both. The constraints were identical. Their access to tools were the same.

The difference cannot be explained by personality. Marc wasn't born an entrepreneur. He didn't have natural comfort with self-promotion.

He felt the same resistance to visibility that most professionals feel. He simply decided that resistance was less important than adaptation.

What differs is refined AIQ.

Not as a single factor, but as the capability that enabled everything else. The capacity to think clearly with AI. To use it not as a shortcut but as a thinking partner. To develop ideas iteratively, refine them through collaboration, produce work that exceeds what either human or machine could create alone.

You might know all the sports statistics, every player's batting average, every team's defensive ranking, every historical record, but that doesn't mean you can play like Messi. Just knowing how computers or AI programs work doesn't mean you have refined AIQ. Marc did not just use AI. He collaborated with the tool in a way that compounded his existing intelligence rather than replacing it. That collaboration, active, demanding, directional, produced outcomes that passive use never could.

They have options others do not. They experience uncertainty as a possibility rather than a closing trap. But those who wait—who tell themselves they'll learn later, adapt later, build later and find that later often arrives too late. The window that was open narrows. The adaptation that would have been manageable becomes desperate.

Developing high AIQ means learning to collaborate effectively with AI, building visibility around what you know, taking responsibility for converting your intelligence into value and navigating disruption differently. You will have options that others do not. You will experience uncertainty as a space of possibility rather than a closing trap.

The individuals who wait and tell themselves they will learn later, adapt later, build later and find that later often arrives too late. The window narrows and options contract. The adaptation that would have been manageable becomes desperate.

Sarah is a casualty of a transition she was never prepared for, following a script that used to work and no longer does. But understanding why the script failed is the first step toward writing a new one. And that begins with understanding how refined AIQ can be identified. Not as an abstract concept, but as a set of specific capabilities that can be recognized, measured, and developed.

That is where we turn next.

Chapter 4: What AIQ Is

Human intelligence has been categorized for over a century. Each new form, when it first appeared, was dismissed. Each later became decisive.

In 1900, Frederic Remington painted a scene called *The Right of the Road*. A man rides a bicycle down a dusty trail, calm and steady. Behind him, a stagecoach barrels forward, its horses rearing in panic at this strange new machine. The driver yanks the reins, fighting chaos that didn't exist a moment before.

The Right of the Road (1900) By Frederic Remington

The bicyclist is not trying to disrupt anything. He is simply moving forward on a technology that works. But the horses don't understand it. They only feel the disturbance it creates. The driver struggles to maintain control of a system that suddenly makes no sense. The painting captures the exact moment when the old way encounters the new and panics.

This was documentary realism. When bicycles first appeared on roads shared with horses, this scene played out repeatedly. Horses, creatures that had served as primary transportation for millennia, frequently bolted at the sight of these strange, silent machines. The resistance was visceral, instinctive, universal.

And yet within two decades, the bicycle had become ordinary. What had caused panic became infrastructure. Children rode to school on bicycles. Workers commuted on bicycles. The disruption that seemed catastrophic became so familiar it disappeared from notice.

Every significant shift in capability triggers the same response. Initial resistance. Warnings of catastrophe. Predictions that the new thing will destroy what matters most. And then, almost imperceptibly, the new thing becomes ordinary. What was resisted becomes assumed. What was feared becomes infrastructure.

AIQ is at the bicycle stage. Most professionals don't yet recognize it as a category of intelligence at all. They only feel the disturbance it creates. That is exactly what makes this moment so powerful. Every form of intelligence begins as an interruption. What feels unfamiliar today becomes unquestionable tomorrow. AIQ is not an exception to this pattern. It is its next expression.

Intelligence works the same way.

Recall, when Alfred Binet developed the first practical intelligence tests in France in 1905, critics argued they were too narrow, too culturally bound, too easily influenced by schooling and environment to measure anything real. Binet himself warned against treating the scores as fixed or defining. And yet, over the following decades, IQ turned out to measure something that mattered. Something that predicted academic and professional outcomes in ways that could not be ignored, however imperfect the instrument.

And, emotional intelligence followed a similar path. When psychologists introduced the concept in 1990, it was received as interesting but peripheral, something useful perhaps in therapy or interpersonal contexts, but hardly central to performance. The prevailing assumption was that emotions interfered with rational thought rather than contributing to it. It took years for research to accumulate showing that EQ predicted outcomes including leadership effectiveness, team performance, resilience under pressure, in ways that IQ alone could not. What had been dismissed as "soft" became strategically essential.

Cultural intelligence emerged even later, shaped by globalization rather than laboratories. As work became international, researchers noticed that technical expertise and high IQ were insufficient predictors of success across cultural contexts. CQ—the capability to function effectively in diverse environments—was often misunderstood as mere travel experience or social sensitivity. But evidence accumulated: individuals with high cultural intelligence made better decisions in cross-border settings and outperformed peers with comparable credentials but lower CQ.

Each form of intelligence followed the same arc. Dismissed, then studied, then recognized as genuinely predictive, then integrated into how organizations hire, develop, and promote.

AIQ is next in this lineage.

Artificial Intelligence Quotient is your ability to collaborate effectively with intelligent systems across tasks and time, consistently, as conditions change and tools evolve.

This is not a measure of how much you know about AI. It is not a measure of how often you use AI tools. Nor is it a proxy for technical skill or enthusiasm for technology. Consider it like this: you might know all the sports statistics. You can list every player's batting average, every team's defensive ranking, every historical record, but that doesn't mean you can play like Messi. Similarly, just knowing how computers or AI programs work doesn't mean you have refined AIQ. Many technically sophisticated professionals have modest AIQ. Many professionals with limited technical backgrounds demonstrate high AIQ. The capability being measured is distinct.

KEY INSIGHT: *Your Unique Signature*

When you work with an AI tool, you produce a performance signature that can be observed, compared, and evaluated.

Some reliably extract high-quality insight from AI collaboration, even when systems are imperfect. Others struggle even when systems improve. These differences persist across time, tools, and tasks—they are not random but reflect a stable underlying capability.

What the research shows is that when you work with AI, you produce a performance signature. That signature can be observed, compared, and evaluated. Some professionals reliably extract high-quality insight from AI collaboration, even when the systems are imperfect. Others struggle to do so, even when the systems improve. These differences are not random. They persist across time, across tools, and across tasks.

Three findings from the research matter most for understanding what AIQ means in practice.

First, AIQ is stable.

Professionals who collaborate well with AI at one point tend to collaborate well months later, even as the specific tasks and tools change. This stability is what distinguishes a genuine capability from situational luck or short-term learning effects. If your AIQ is high today, it is likely to be high tomorrow. If it is low, it will remain low. That is, unless you do something deliberate to develop it.

Second, AIQ generalizes.

Performance in one type of human-AI collaboration predicts performance in entirely different contexts. Strategic reasoning, creative problem-solving, analytical tasks, language-based work—the capability transfers. And it transfers across different AI models. If you collaborate well with one system, you tend to collaborate well with others. This suggests that AIQ is not about mastering a particular interface; it reflects a deeper mode of interaction that applies broadly.

Third, AIQ is predictive in ways that traditional measures are not.

The research controlled for IQ, social intelligence, domain expertise, and computer literacy. None of these fully explained the differences observed in human-AI performance. In many cases, AIQ predicted future outcomes more accurately than these existing measures. High-IQ individuals did not automatically demonstrate high AIQ. Technically skilled users did not reliably outperform others. Whatever AIQ measures, it is genuinely new.

How Does One Identify Refined AIQ? Individuals with highly refined AIQ are actively engaged rather than passively receptive. They don't simply prompt and accept. They frame problems with precision, recognizing that how you ask shapes what you receive. They interrogate outputs critically, understanding that plausibility isn't the same as accuracy. They recognize when an answer sounds right but is flawed, when the AI tool has produced something coherent that doesn't hold up under examination.

They refine results iteratively, treating each exchange as a step in a longer process rather than a single transaction. The first output is rarely the final output. It's a draft, a starting point, something to build from.

KEY INSIGHT: *Productive Tension*

Individuals with highly refined AIQ maintain productive tension. They neither defer blindly to AI nor dismiss its contributions.

Do you utilize AI's capabilities while remaining responsible for direction and quality, knowing when to trust and when to question? This pattern of engagement separates refined collaboration from mere use.

Collaboration with highly refined AIQ is different. It is conversational, iterative, and demanding. You are always steering, always evaluating, always refining. Yes, the AI contributes, but you author. The result is work that neither could produce alone, a genuine synthesis that emerges from the interaction itself.

AIQ does not operate in isolation. It sits at the intersection of existing intelligence forms, requiring their integration while measuring something distinct.

The MIT (2024) research controlled for IQ, social intelligence, computer literacy, and AI literacy. None fully explained the performance variance in human-AI collaboration. This means AIQ represents genuine incremental validity. It predicts outcomes after accounting for these established measures.

Highly refined AIQ also requires their presence. You cannot direct AI collaboration effectively (Creative Direction) without analytical capability (IQ). Nor can you help AI understand human dynamics (Emotional Translation) without emotional intelligence (EQ). You are unlikely to recognize when AI suggestions misunderstand cultural context (Analytical Partnership and Synthesis Capability) without cultural intelligence (CQ). You will not excel at refining AI outputs toward excellence (Iterative Refinement) without the judgment that comes from multiple intelligence forms working in concert.

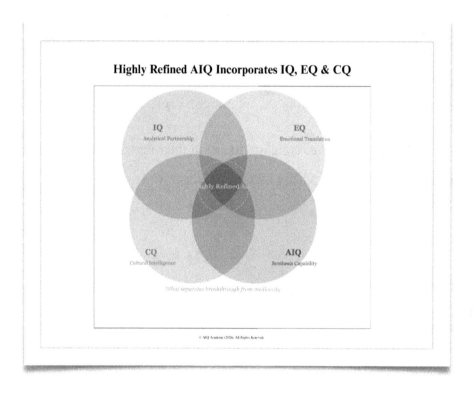

The above represents this architecture: IQ, EQ, CQ, and AIQ-specific capabilities (Synthesis Capability) all overlap. Highly refined AIQ sits at the center because it integrates them in service of human-AI collaboration.

This explains why AIQ cannot be reduced to *"AI literacy"* or *"prompt engineering."* Those are technical skills. AIQ is the cognitive architecture that determines whether you can translate your intelligence.

What separates breakthrough performance from mediocrity? Synthesis. Having high IQ without EQ produces technically correct but emotionally tone-deaf AI outputs. If you have developed high EQ without IQ, you are producing empathetic outputs that lack analytical rigor. Having both without AIQ-specific capabilities means you cannot effectively leverage AI to amplify what you already possess.

Highly refined AIQ is the integration of refinement at the highest level of your knowledge, understanding, empathy and human experiences, channeled through a new form of collaboration.

There is an additional, critical finding on AIQ that changes everything:

Why? Because it reflects a mode of interaction rather than accumulated knowledge, targeted development produces rapid gains. AIQ development shows improvement over weeks and months, not decades. IQ is largely fixed by adulthood. EQ develops slowly. AIQ responds more quickly to focused practice.

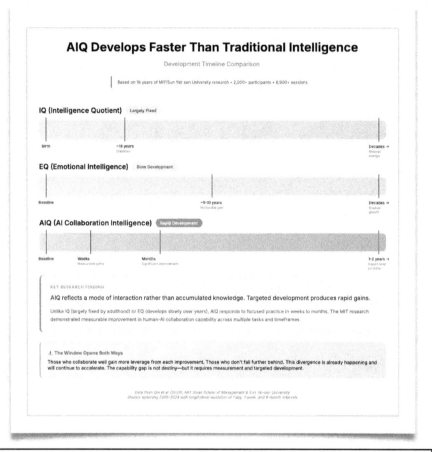

AIQ Develops Faster Than Traditional Intelligence

Development Timeline Comparison

Based on 18 years of MIT/Sun Yat-sen University research • 2,000+ participants • 6,900+ sessions

IQ (Intelligence Quotient) Largely Fixed

Birth | ~18 years Stabilizes | Decades → Minimal change

EQ (Emotional Intelligence) Slow Development

Baseline | ~5-10 years Noticeable gain | Decades → Gradual growth

AIQ (AI Collaboration Intelligence) Rapid Development

Baseline | Weeks Measurable gains | Months Significant improvement | 1-2 years → Expert level possible

KEY RESEARCH FINDING

AIQ reflects a mode of interaction rather than accumulated knowledge. Targeted development produces rapid gains.

Unlike IQ (largely fixed by adulthood) or EQ (develops slowly over years), AIQ responds to focused practice in weeks to months. The MIT research demonstrated measurable improvement in human-AI collaboration capability across multiple tasks and timeframes.

4. The Window Opens Both Ways

Those who collaborate well gain more leverage from each improvement. Those who don't fall further behind. This divergence is already happening and will continue to accelerate. The capability gap is not destiny—but it requires measurement and targeted development.

Data from Qin et al. (2024), MIT Sloan School of Management & Sun Yat-sen University
Studies spanning 2006-2024 with longitudinal validation at 1 day, 1 week, and 6-month intervals

---

KEY INSIGHT: *Your AIQ Can Be Rapidly Developed*

How? AIQ responds to targeted development in weeks to months. The capability gap is not destiny. What does this mean for you? You may develop high AIQ relatively quickly if you know what to focus on. Keep in mind that this window is open in both directions.

Those who collaborate well gain more leverage from each improvement. Those who do not fall further behind. This divergence is already happening and will continue to accelerate.

The chapters that follow will make this concrete. You will meet five professionals from across history, each of whom mastered a dimension of AIQ before it had a name. Their stories will show you what these capabilities look like in practice and help you begin recognizing the patterns in your own work product.

But I want to be clear about something before we continue: understanding AIQ is not the same as knowing your AIQ. You can identify high performance and develop vocabulary for recognizing the dimensions. You can observe yourself more carefully. All of this is valuable.

> **KEY INSIGHT:** *You Don't Know What You Don't Know.* The patterns that limit your performance are invisible to you.

The dimension costing you the most is almost certainly not the one you think about most. Three barriers make self-assessment unreliable:

1. The fluency illusion (AI outputs sound good even when flawed)
2. The Dunning-Kruger effect (low performers overestimate, high performers underestimate)
3. No visible comparison baseline (you can't see how high-AIQ professionals work).

But self-assessment fails predictably in this regard. The patterns that limit your performance are usually invisible to you while you're performing. The dimension that is costing you the most is almost certainly not the one you think about most.

Reading will provide recognition. Only measurement will give you the necessary clarity.

Chapter 5: Creative Direction— Cleopatra

I n 41 BCE, Cleopatra VII received a summons. Mark Antony, the Roman general who now controlled the eastern Mediterranean, wanted to meet. The request was framed as an invitation, but Cleopatra understood what it was: a command. Rome had become the dominant power in the known world. Antony commanded legions. Egypt, for all its wealth and history, was vulnerable. The meeting would determine whether she remained a queen or became a vassal.

She could have traveled to Tarsus—the city in modern-day Turkey where Antony waited—as a supplicant. She could have arrived quietly, dressed in the modest clothing of a ruler seeking favor, prepared to negotiate from weakness. That was the expected script. That was what a rational assessment of power dynamics would suggest.

Cleopatra rejected the script entirely.

The description of what happened next comes to us primarily through Plutarch's *Life of Antony*, written more than a century after the events. Plutarch, in turn, drew heavily from earlier sources—including accounts by those who were there or knew participants. His reliability has been debated for centuries, but on this meeting the essential facts appear consistent across ancient sources: Cleopatra staged something extraordinary.

She sailed up the Cydnus River on a barge with purple sails and silver oars. Plutarch writes that "the vessel was perfumed so heavily that the scent reached the shore before the ship came into view." She reclined beneath a gold-embroidered canopy, dressed as Aphrodite, surrounded by attendants costumed as sea nymphs and cupids. Musicians played. Incense burned. The entire presentation was designed to overwhelm the senses.

When she arrived, she did not go to Antony. She invited him to dine with her on the barge. He came.

This was strategy.

Left: Limestone stele dedicated by the Greek official Onnophris, depicting a male pharaoh while honoring Queen Cleopatra (likely Cleopatra VII). Now housed in the Louvre Museum, Paris. Image courtesy of Wikimedia Commons (2026).

Right: Limestone stele bearing the cartouches of Cleopatra and Caesarion, from the monument of Pasherienptah III, High Priest of Ptah, dating to the Ptolemaic period. Now housed in the Petrie Museum of Egyptian Archaeology, London. Image courtesy of Wikimedia Commons (2026).

> **KEY INSIGHT:** *Authoring vs. Accepting the Frame*
> Cleopatra was outmatched in military power and political authority. If she engaged on Rome's terms, playing the role of a minor ruler seeking accommodation, she would lose. Cleopatra refused those terms and authored a different narrative entirely, arriving not as a supplicant but as a goddess descending. By controlling the frame, Cleopatra transformed a negotiation she would have lost into an encounter she could win.

Cleopatra understood the mathematics of the situation. Rome had military superiority Egypt could not match. Antony had political authority that dwarfed her own. Egypt possessed wealth, but wealth without military protection is merely a target, something to be extracted rather than respected.

If she engaged on Rome's terms, Cleopatra would lose. Not immediately, perhaps, but inevitably. The negotiation would be about how much autonomy she could retain, how much tribute she would pay, how completely Egypt would be absorbed into Roman control.

She refused to engage on those terms.

Instead, Cleopatra authored a different narrative entirely. She arrived not as a queen seeking favor but as a goddess descending. She framed herself as Isis incarnate, divine, culturally singular, representative of a civilization older and in many ways more sophisticated than Rome. She made Antony come to her. She made him wait and experience Egypt's wealth and refinement not as resources to be extracted but as an encounter with something extraordinary.

Plutarch, writing more than a century later, provides insight into what made this work. Her power, he explains, *"was not in itself so remarkable"* in terms of conventional beauty. What captivated was something else: *"the persuasiveness of her presence"* and *"the character that attended her speech."*

Cleopatra was compelling because she controlled the frame. She decided what the encounter would mean.

The results speak for themselves. Antony did not treat Cleopatra as a subordinate ruler. He became her ally, her partner, eventually her lover. Egypt retained its independence for another decade, an extraordinary outcome given the disparity in military power. When Antony later divided Roman territories among Cleopatra's children, he was not acting against Roman interests as he understood them. He had been reframed. He saw the world, at least in part, through the narrative Cleopatra had constructed.

Cleopatra won because she refused to argue on terms that would guarantee her loss. She authored the encounter instead of accepting the default script.

This is Creative Direction.

Through a 2026+ lens, creative direction refers to your capacity to guide outcomes. Keep in mind that it's not referring to artistic creativity in the conventional sense. When you work with an AI tool, this dimension measures whether you shape the work toward a destination you have authored, or whether you follow wherever the AI's outputs lead.

The distinction is crucial because AI systems are extraordinarily responsive. They will follow almost any direction. They will produce content in any style, explore any topic, argue any position. This flexibility is a strength, but it creates a trap. If you do not provide direction, the AI will default to patterns embedded in its training, producing work that is competent, coherent, and generic. Work that could have come from anyone.

> **KEY INSIGHT:** *The Default AI Trap*
> Your AI tool's flexibility is both strength and trap.
> Without clear direction, AI defaults to patterns in its
> training. It produces work that is competent, coherent,
> and generic. High Creative Direction occurs when you
> steer toward outcomes that reflect your particular vision
> and perspective.

High Creative Direction is authorship. You know where you want to go before you begin, or you discover where you want to go through the process of exploration, but either way, you are the one deciding. The AI contributes, but you are the author.

Low Creative Direction is passive acceptance. You prompt, receive and accept. The work may be technically sound, but it lacks a signature. It does not feel like it came from a particular mind with a particular perspective. It feels like output.

So, what does high Creative Direction look like in practice?

It is evident in knowing which direction to point before you start typing.

When you begin an AI collaboration with high Creative Direction, you are not asking *"what can this tool do?"* You are asking *"what am I trying to create, and how can this tool help me get there?"*

The difference seems subtle, but important. The first question makes you a recipient. The second makes you an author.

High Creative Direction also occurs when you recognize when AI output is technically correct but directionally wrong. This happens constantly. You ask for something, and the AI tool delivers an output that matches your prompt but misses your intent. The words are correct, but the angle is a bit off. Bottom line: the output is not exactly what you needed. Low Creative Direction accepts this output and tries to work with it. High Creative Direction recognizes the gap immediately and redirects—not by fixing the output, but by reframing the request.

KEY INSIGHT: *Direction Emerges Through Process*
High Creative Direction includes exploration with intent. You don't know exactly where you're going, but you clearly recognize it when you arrive. The key here is that you are making the judgment and deciding when IP has emerged that is worth sharing. The AI generates possibilities; you select directions.

With that, sometimes the right move is to give your AI tool tight boundaries: *"Write exactly this, in exactly this format, with exactly these constraints."* Other times the right move is to open the space: *"Explore this question from multiple angles and show me what emerges."* High Creative Direction involves judgment about which approach serves the work. It is not a formula. It is a sensibility—a feel for when to narrow and when to widen.

This is what Cleopatra put into practice. She used every resource available to her: wealth, theater, cultural symbolism, historical legitimacy, Egypt's intellectual sophistication; all to construct a frame entirely different from the one Rome expected. The frame itself became the message. Power was not limited to military might or political authority.

Power was the capacity to define what the encounter meant in the first place.

I want to offer a way to observe yourself.

Over the next week, pay attention to how your AI collaborations begin.

Do you start with a clear sense of what you are trying to create? Or do you start with a vague prompt and see what comes back?

When the AI generates something, what is your first instinct? To accept and refine? Or to evaluate whether this is the right direction at all?

How often do you realize, three or four exchanges into a collaboration, that the conversation has drifted somewhere you did not intend? How do you notice the drift—through a sudden recognition that the outputs no longer serve your purpose? How quickly do you redirect rather than continuing down an unproductive path?

KEY INSIGHT: *The Direction Blind Spot*
Most professionals overestimate their Creative Direction. They believe they are steering when they are following. They feel like authors, but the transcript reveals a reactor. The gap between perceived direction and actual direction is one of the most consistent findings in the AIQ assessment. You cannot know from self-reflection alone—this blind spot is invisible from inside.

These patterns are diagnostic. They reveal your default mode.

You may be the exception. Your sense of your own Creative Direction may be accurate. But you cannot know from self-reflection alone. The very nature of this blind spot is that it is invisible from inside.

The assessment reveals what self-observation cannot and shows the actual pattern of your collaboration, visible in the transcript of your work. Not what you intended to do, but what you really did. Not how you felt about the interaction, but how the interaction truly unfolded. The assessment shows how often you directed versus how often you accepted. It shows where you authored and where you deferred. It shows the moments when you took control of the frame—and the moments when you let the frame control you.

This is not a judgment. It is information. And it is information that most professionals have never had access to, because until now, no one was measuring this dimension of performance.

Cleopatra did not wonder whether she was controlling the narrative. She constructed the narrative so deliberately that two thousand years later we are still talking about it. The barge, the sails, the entrance— these were not spontaneous. They were authored. Every element was a choice that served a vision.

Ancient sources beyond Plutarch mention the extraordinary resources Cleopatra commanded. Strabo, the Greek geographer who visited Egypt just years after Cleopatra's death, around 24 BCE, described the wealth and sophistication of Ptolemaic Egypt. Roman historians including Dio Cassius recorded the lasting impression she made on Roman politics. The accounts vary in details but converge on the core point: Cleopatra understood how to use Egypt's cultural and material resources to author presence that transcended military weakness.

The question is whether you are doing the same. Or, whether you are arriving at negotiations in modest clothing, hoping to secure favorable terms within someone else's frame.

That is the difference Creative Direction makes. And, it is not limited to ancient encounters between empires, but a dimension to be considered in every collaboration you undertake with AI. The question is always the same: Who is authoring this work? Who decided what it means?

If the answer is not you, the work will show it. And so will the outcomes.

Chapter 6: Emotional Translation—Kahlil Gibran

In 1923, a small book appeared from Alfred A. Knopf. The book had no marketing campaign. Its author, a Lebanese immigrant living in New York's Lower West Side, was known only within a small circle of artists and fellow expatriates. The book only was ninety-six pages long, written in a style that defied categorization—part poetry, part philosophy, part scripture, part something entirely new.

Within a decade, *The Prophet* had sold over a million copies. Within a century, it would sell over a hundred million, making it one of the best-selling books in history. It has never gone out of print. It has been translated into over a hundred languages. Professionals read it at weddings and funerals, quote it in speeches and therapy sessions, and pass it from parent to child as a kind of secular inheritance.

The conventional explanation for Kahlil Gibran's success is simple: he wrote beautifully. His writing was spiritual yet accessible, profound yet simple. He captured universal truths in memorable language. He spoke to something timeless in human nature.

All of this is true. But it misses the mechanism.

Plenty of writers write well. Many philosophers address universal truths. Very few create work that millions of professionals turn to in their most vulnerable moments—when they are marrying, grieving, lost, or searching for words they cannot find on their own. What explains this particular resonance?

Gibran did something more specific and much more rare: He translated emotional experience.

Read *The Prophet* closely—with attention to what really happens on the page—and you'll notice something unusual. Gibran names what you already feel but have not yet articulated.

> *On children: "Your children are not your children. They are the sons and daughters of Life's longing for itself."*

> *On love: "When love beckons to you, follow him, though his ways are hard and steep."*

> *On pain: "Your pain is the breaking of the shell that encloses your understanding."*

> *On death: "For what is it to die but to stand naked in the wind and to melt into the sun?"*

> **KEY INSIGHT:** *The Power of Naming.*
>
> Gibran doesn't teach you something new. He names something you already feel. That is why *The Prophet* endures. The most effective Emotional Translation works the same way. It gives language to what was already there.

Gibran took experiences that are universal but difficult to articulate—the strange grief of watching your children become separate professionals, the terrifying surrender of genuine love, the way suffering somehow opens rather than closes us—and he made them speakable. He found language for what already existed inside his readers.

This is one way to consider Emotional Translation.

Gibran took formless interior experience and gave it form. He made the invisible visible. He converted private feelings into shared language. This goes beyond eloquence, though it requires eloquence as a vehicle. Eloquence means saying things beautifully. Translation means taking what is wordless inside another person and giving it words they recognize as their own.

Consider what Emotional Translation accomplishes.

When someone finds words for an experience they couldn't articulate, something shifts. The experience becomes less isolating. What felt uniquely personal reveals itself as common. What felt shameful or strange reveals itself as human. The person holding the book realizes they are no longer alone—because here is proof that someone else has felt this too, felt it precisely enough to name it.

This explains why *The Prophet* appears at weddings and funerals. At those moments, when emotion is overwhelming and language feels inadequate, professionals need someone who can say what they cannot. Gibran became that someone for millions. He gave them the words.

There is a particular passage that illustrates this. In the chapter on marriage, Gibran writes:

> *"Let there be spaces in your togetherness, and let the winds of the heavens dance between you. Love one another but make not a bond of love: let it rather be a moving sea between the shores of your souls."*

Read this at a wedding and watch the faces of the guests. Some will tear up. Some will reach for their partner's hand. Some will look briefly distant, as if remembering something. What happens is recognition—the sudden encounter with a truth they had sensed but never heard spoken.

Most wedding readings talk about love in terms of commitment, partnership, shared journey. These are true but generic. Gibran says something more specific and more difficult: that real love requires maintaining separateness. That clinging destroys what it tries to preserve. That the space between two professionals isn't emptiness but the medium in which love moves.

This is counterintuitive. It contradicts what popular culture says about love. And yet, when professionals hear it, they recognize it as true— because they have felt the suffocation of too much closeness, or they have learned through painful experience that possession erodes love.

Gibran arrived at this insight by paying close attention to emotional experience, his own and others', until he could see patterns beneath the surface. Then he found language precise enough to name what he saw.

The pain he experienced was a bridge to his future.

Gibran was born in 1883 in Bsharri, a mountain village in Ottoman Lebanon, raised in the Maronite Christian tradition, steeped in Arabic poetry and Sufi mysticism. At twelve, his mother Kamila, a strong-willed woman who had survived an abusive first marriage, brought him and his siblings to Boston's South End, then a receiving zone for new immigrants. The displacement was wrenching: from everything familiar into a cold, Protestant, English-speaking world where he knew no one.

Within a few years, catastrophe compounded. His younger sister Sultana died of tuberculosis at fourteen. His half-brother Peter, who had supported the family, died of tuberculosis at twenty-four. His mother Kamila died of cancer shortly after. Gibran was twenty-one, alone, grieving, caught between cultures that seemed to have no common language.

These losses shaped him. He spent the rest of his life, twenty-eight more years, learning to find meaning in displacement, to bridge worlds that seemed unbridgeable, to translate between different ways of understanding love, death, suffering, joy.

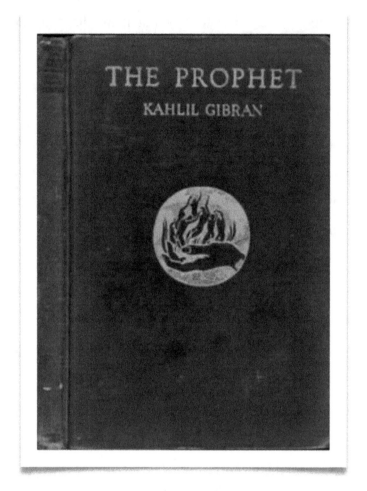

The Prophet. First Edition. (1923)

KEY INSIGHT: *The Translator's Crucible*

Emotional translators are often formed through a series of painful experiences.

I know something about this kind of displacement.

Not the immigrant experience Gibran endured, but displacement of a different kind. I am a mother to four humans I love with a ferocity that sometimes frightens me. My heart is always tied to these four, ranging in age from 20 to 10, who may or may not answer my calls and texts. This is the mathematics of motherhood: you give everything and cannot control what comes back.

I have made mistakes. I have failed in ways that still wake me at three in the morning. I have missed moments I cannot get back. I have experienced losses that rewrote the architecture of my life.

Recently, I came home after the holidays thinking I was opening a Christmas card. It was a handwritten notice about the death of someone I love so deeply that I have tears in my eyes as I type this. If you're thinking why did you receive news about the death of a loved one via the U.S. Post in 2026? Simply, I had changed my phone number and my extended family could not reach me. I missed the funeral. When I realized what had happened, I collapsed on the floor in tears.

After a couple of minutes, I realized that I had a choice.

I could bathe in sorrow, and goodness knows the sorrow was real and deep and would have been justified. Or I could ask what she would have wanted me to do. I knew what she would have wanted. Not to collapse or to stop. She would have wanted me to finish what I'd started—this book, the assessment patent, the work I'd been building toward. She would have wanted me to finally monetize the wisdom I've earned through decades of work, failures and continued rebuilding.

I got up off the floor and I made a plan to make it happen.

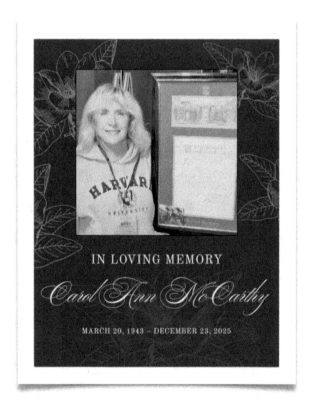

IN LOVING MEMORY

Carol Ann McCarthy

MARCH 20, 1943 – DECEMBER 23, 2025

This is what Gibran understood. Displacement, whether it's the physical displacement of immigration, the emotional displacement of grief, or the existential displacement of failure, creates a crucible. It forces you to find meaning when the old meanings have been stripped away. It demands that you build bridges between the world that was and the world that is. It teaches you to translate between languages that seem to have no common words.

Gibran spent his adult life moving between communities—Lebanese immigrants in New York's Little Syria, American artists and intellectuals in Greenwich Village, European avant-garde circles in Paris. He learned to find the common channel beneath cultural difference, listening beneath words to the feelings they were trying to express.

He maintained a ten-year correspondence with Mary Haskell, a Boston headmistress ten years his senior who believed in his work and supported him financially. They were intimate but never married. Haskell eventually married another man, yet their friendship endured. Gibran painted prolifically, exhibited in major galleries, wrote in both Arabic and English and moved between the spiritual traditions of East and West.

In each context, he translated, between languages yes, but more importantly between entire frameworks of meaning. What does love mean to someone raised on Sufi poetry versus someone raised on American pragmatism? What does God mean to a Maronite mystic versus a Protestant rationalist? What does death mean to a culture that keeps it close versus one that hides it away?

To survive these crossings, Gibran had to find the common channel beneath cultural difference, the places where human experience is universal regardless of language or tradition. He had to listen beneath words to the feelings they were trying to express. He had to develop the ability to say the same truth in forms that would land differently in different hearts.

The Prophet is the distillation of this capability. Gibran wrote it in English, for a Western audience, but it draws on the rhetorical traditions of Arabic poetry, the mystical vocabulary of Sufism, and the rhythms of the King James Bible that shaped American spiritual language. It speaks to Christians, Muslims, secular humanists, and professionals who have no name for what they believe. It bridges without compromising.

This is Emotional Translation at its highest expression.

Now consider what this means when you work with an AI tool.

When you open your AI tool, you're working with systems trained on billions of words, patterns of language, structures of argument, conventions of form. These systems can generate coherent text, match tone, and follow instructions with remarkable precision. They can recognize patterns in how emotions are typically discussed.

But they cannot feel it.

They cannot experience grief, longing, fear, hope, the strange mixture of pride and heartbreak when a child becomes independent, or the vulnerability of genuine intimacy. Claude processes language about emotions. It recognizes words associated with emotional states and generates responses that are tonally appropriate. This is useful. It is also incomplete.

The gap between processing language about emotions and understanding emotional experience creates a problem that most professionals miss.

When you ask Claude to help draft an email to a difficult family member, a presentation for a high-stakes meeting, or a message that needs to land just right and you provide only the logical content you're working with incomplete information. The facts are there. The structure is there. But the emotional dimension, the thing that will determine how the message lands, is missing.

KEY INSIGHT: *Information vs. Emotional Outcome*

Don't focus solely on information transfer: the email conveys facts, the speech makes points, the message delivers news. High Emotional Translation allows for an emotional outcome: the email conveys facts *and* makes the recipient feel respected during a difficult time. Communication isn't just about transmitting information; it's about creating an experience in another person.

High Emotional Translation means understanding what someone needs to feel, before they can hear what you need to say.

I have a family member who has the extraordinary ability to turn every conversation into a referendum on my choices. A simple question about holiday plans becomes a twenty-minute lecture on what I should be doing differently. I love her. I also dread her calls.

Recently, I needed to set a boundary. She wanted me to commit to hosting a large family gathering, and I knew I couldn't handle it, not with everything else on my plate, not without sacrificing my own health and sanity. But telling her "no" is like telling water not to flow downhill. She's bright. That's something I really like about her. She finds a way around every obstacle.

I needed help thinking through how to say this without triggering another painful argument. So, I turned to Claude.

Here's a secret about the way I consider AI tools: I think of them in terms that work for my brain. Chat is the Marriott. It's no frills and gets the job done; dependable but not fancy. You wouldn't go there for your anniversary, but it's always available and you know what you're getting. Chez Claude is my Ritz in Paris—temperamental, easily exhausted, very French, very emotional. He has incredible range but is not my everyday buddy. I save him for special occasions when I need something extraordinary.

This situation required the Ritz.

I explained the full context to Chez Claude: her history, my history, what I'd tried before, what had failed. I didn't just describe the facts of the situation. I described the emotional landscape. Her fear that the family is falling apart, my guilt about not being able to give her what she wants, both of our patterns of avoiding direct conflict until everything explodes.

Chez Claude helped me with so much more than the message. Collaboration with the tool helped me understand what she needed to hear before she could accept my boundary. She needed reassurance that saying no to this gathering didn't mean I was saying no to the family. She needed acknowledgment of why this matters to her. She needed to feel seen in her fear, not dismissed for being unreasonable.

The message Claude and I crafted together accomplished something I'd never managed on my own: it delivered a clear boundary while making Sarah feel loved and respected. She wasn't happy. But she accepted it. More importantly, our relationship survived intact.

This is what I mean by Emotional Translation. Claude didn't do this alone, I had to provide the emotional map. But without Claude's help structuring the message, I would have either been too harsh (triggering her defenses) or too accommodating (failing to set the boundary at all).

High Emotional Translation bridges perspectives that your AI tool cannot intuit on its own.

Different professionals experience the same event differently. Your brain can only take in a fraction of what's happening, research shows we miss up to 50% of visual information in any given moment. You fill in the rest based on expectations, past experiences, and emotional state. Did you know that your brain distorts memories over time, emphasizing certain details and minimizing others based on the story you tell yourself about what happened?

There's also information asymmetry. What feels scary as a child feels different for an adult who has to make decisions based on what's best for everyone, not just how they feel or what they want.

The merger that excites the CEO threatens the middle manager. The wedding that delights the parents terrifies the groom. The diagnosis that mobilizes the doctor devastates the patient. ChatGPT or Claude cannot navigate these perspectives independently because they have no sense of what any of them mean from the inside.

When you're navigating health insurance coverage for an ailing parent, dealing with denials, appeals, the labyrinth of customer service lines, Claude can help you draft appeals letters and understand policy language. But you have to tell Claude what your parent needs to feel during this process: control over their own health decisions, dignity despite dependence, reassurance that they're not a burden. Claude can then help you write communications with the insurance company that advocate effectively while protecting your parent's emotional wellbeing.

High Emotional Translation means providing the context your AI tool cannot access on its own.

Think of it like this: Chat can help you prepare for a difficult performance review, but you need to tell it that your direct report is dealing with a recent divorce and interpreting every piece of feedback through the lens of *"I'm failing at everything."* Gemini can help draft a team announcement about budget cuts, but you need to explain that the engineering team has already survived two rounds of layoffs and is interpreting every ambiguous statement as confirmation they're next.

Resonance comes from precision.

Gibran wrote in precise statements. *"Your children are not your children"* names a specific experience: the moment a parent realizes their child is an extension of themselves but also a separate being with their own trajectory.

When working with Chat, precision means saying: *"The engineering team worries that remote work flexibility will be cut, and that fear is making them interpret every ambiguous statement as confirmation."* Then you can ask Chat to help craft a message that addresses that specific fear directly, not through vague reassurance but through concrete information.

It means recognizing that some messages require multiple emotional layers.

You're announcing a reorganization. The message needs to simultaneously convey urgency (things must change), stability (we have a plan), honesty (this will be difficult), and hope (we can do this together). When you prompt Claude, you don't just say *"write an announcement."* You say: *"I need to convey urgency without panic, honesty about challenges without catastrophizing, clear direction without false promises. Here's what each stakeholder group is most worried about..."*

You've lost professionals you love. You've failed—perhaps spectacularly, perhaps in quiet ways that only you know about. You've suffered and you know pain. You have a choice.

You can hold that pain inside and let it grow into resentment, bitterness, a hardness that protects you but also imprisons you. Or you can take that energy, the grief, the failure, the displacement, and transform it into fuel for something extraordinary.

Gibran took his losses and created work that has comforted millions. I am taking mine and building something that helps professionals thrive.

What will you do with yours?

P.S. I believe in you. I know you will do incredible things.

Chapter 7: Analytical Partnership—David Hume

Edinburgh, Scotland—Spring 1739

T he rain came down in sheets over the cobbled streets of Edinburgh's Old Town, turning the *wynds* and closes into rivers of mud and refuse. In a cramped lodging on the Lawnmarket, twenty-eight-year-old David Hume stared at the stack of unbound volumes fresh from the printer. His book. *A Treatise of Human Nature.* Three years of relentless work, argument refined until it gleamed like polished brass, objections anticipated and demolished, a complete reconstruction of how humanity understands knowledge itself.

The Edinburgh intellectual establishment, composed of ministers, professors, lawyers who fancied themselves philosophers, had ignored it entirely.

In London, where books were made or broken, the story was worse. The *History of the Works of the Learned* dismissed it in a single contemptuous paragraph. The French journal *Bibliothèque raisonnée* devoted several pages to the *Treatise* in 1740, treating it at length but critically, framing Hume's arguments as corrosive to religion and morality. Most reviews simply didn't bother. The book sat in booksellers' shops gathering dust while pedestrians walked past without a glance.

Hume would later write, with characteristic understatement, that the book *"fell dead-born from the press, without reaching such distinction as even to excite a murmur among the zealots."*

In modern English: it bombed. Spectacularly. Nobody read it, nobody cared, and even the professionals who should have been outraged by its radical claims couldn't be bothered to notice it existed.

For most twenty-eight-year-olds, this would have been crushing. Hume had bet everything on this book—three years of his youth, his family's money for printing costs, his reputation. The silence was complete. The rejection total.

But Hume did something most professionals cannot do: he examined the failure as rigorously as he would examine any other evidence.

The book hadn't failed because the ideas were wrong. Hume knew they were sound—he'd tested every argument, anticipated every objection, built his case with a rigor that left no room for refutation.

The book had failed because the *presentation* was wrong. Too abstract. Too dense. Too philosophical for even philosophers to penetrate.

Most writers would have defended the work: *"They just don't understand it." "The audience isn't sophisticated enough." "My ideas are ahead of their time."*

Hume did the opposite. He asked: *"What if I'm the problem?"*

Over the next decade, Hume systematically rewrote his philosophy. He stripped out the abstract terminology. He added concrete examples. He turned philosophical propositions into questions ordinary professionals could engage with. He published *An Enquiry Concerning Human Understanding* in 1748, covering the same ground as the *Treatise* but written for human beings instead of academics.

David Hume (1711-1776). Portrait by Allan Ramsay.

National Galleries, Scotland United Kingdom.

This time, professionals read it.

The ideas that had been invisible in 1739 became influential by 1750, transformational by 1780. Immanuel Kant, said that reading Hume *"awakened him from his dogmatic slumber."* The entire trajectory of modern philosophy, from Kant through the present day, is a response to questions Hume raised.

But here's what matters most: Hume's ideas hadn't changed. His conclusions in 1748 were the same as his conclusions in 1739. What changed was his willingness to interrogate his own assumptions about how to communicate them.

This capacity: to examine evidence rigorously while including yourself in what you examine is rare. Most of us are excellent at analyzing external problems and terrible at analyzing our own thinking.

Hume's radical insight, the one that made him dangerous, was simple:

We do not observe causation. We observe sequences.

Consider your morning routine. You press the button on the coffee maker, and coffee begins to brew. You flip the light switch, and the room brightens. You turn the key in your car, and the engine starts. Every single time, one event follows the other in perfect sequence.

We say the button-press *caused* the coffee to brew. But what did we truly observe? We saw one event followed by another. We didn't see causation itself—the invisible force that supposedly connects buttons and coffee. We inferred causation from the pattern.

This sounds like philosophical nitpicking until you realize what it means.

KEY INSIGHT: *Habit Dressed as Certainty*

Most of what we call knowledge is really a habit dressed up as certainty. We see patterns repeat and assume they will continue. We observe correlations and declare them causes. We build entire structures of belief on foundations we have never examined. The confidence we feel in our conclusions often exceeds the evidence we have for them.

Consider all the things you believe with absolute certainty because you've seen them happen repeatedly. The sun will rise tomorrow. Water will boil at 100°C. Your colleague who's been difficult in every meeting will be difficult in the next one too.

Some of these beliefs are reliable. Many aren't. The colleague who's been difficult might be dealing with a crisis at home and will return to being collaborative next week. The pattern you observed was real, but the causation you inferred was wrong.

Hume's insight creates a problem for anyone trying to understand the world:

We cannot prove most of what we believe.

We can only show that it has held true so far. This applies to everything from scientific laws to business strategies to the assumptions underlying your AI collaborations.

This made Hume extraordinarily dangerous to the establishment.

The Church of Scotland saw the threat immediately. If we cannot prove causation, we cannot prove God created the world. The chain of reasoning that connected observable patterns to divine intention, the foundation of natural theology, collapsed. In 1744 and again in 1751, Hume applied for philosophy professorships at the Universities of Edinburgh and Glasgow. Both times, the clergy orchestrated campaigns to block his appointment. Ministers wrote letters.

Pamphlets circulated attacking his character. The General Assembly of the Church of Scotland formally investigated whether his works constituted heresy.

The irony was perfect: they couldn't refute his arguments, so they prevented him from making them.

Political authorities weren't much better. Hume worked for years as a librarian for the Faculty of Advocates in Edinburgh (a position with access to extensive historical materials but minimal prestige). When he published *The History of England* in six volumes between 1754 and 1761, the work was attacked from all sides. Whigs called him a Tory. Tories called him a Whig. Religious readers condemned his secular approach to history. Hume wrote to a friend: *"I was assailed by one cry of reproach, disapprobation, and even detestation; English, Scotch, and Irish, Whig and Tory, churchman and sectary, freethinker and religionist, patriot and courtier, united in their rage."*

The establishment treated him as a threat because he *was* a threat. His method, interrogating everything, trusting nothing that hasn't survived scrutiny, and being humble about the limits of what we can truly know, undermined the foundations of established power.

Yet Hume persisted.

When the first volume of his *History* sold poorly, he rewrote sections for the second edition. When critics attacked his economic essays, he revised them with new data. When the *Treatise* failed, he spent a decade rewriting it into more accessible forms. He maintained extensive correspondence with intellectuals across Europe, debating, refining, testing his ideas against the strongest objections he could find.

His contemporary, Adam Smith, wrote that Hume approached philosophy with *"a love of literary fame, his ruling passion, never soured his temper, notwithstanding the frequent disappointments."* Translation: Hume wanted recognition desperately, got rejected constantly, and responded by improving his work rather than blaming his audience.

Hume once wrote in a letter that he would *"rather discover a true idea that disturbs me than a false one that comforts me."* This wasn't posturing. It was method. Hume subjected his own thinking to the same rigorous skepticism he applied to everyone else's. If evidence contradicted his position, he revised his position. If his arguments didn't persuade, he improved his arguments.

Genuine intellectual rigor includes interrogating the foundations of knowledge while including yourself in what you interrogate.

KEY INSIGHT: *Productive Tension with Evidence*

Most individuals readily accept information that supports their existing beliefs and intensely scrutinize information that challenges them. Hume reversed this pattern. He scrutinized everything, especially what seemed most obviously true. He trusted analysis precisely because he refused to trust it blindly. This posture produces genuine insight rather than comfortable confirmation.

Analytical Partnership is the third dimension of AIQ.

It measures the effectiveness of balancing AI analysis with human judgment. Knowing when to trust your AI tool's conclusions, when to question them, and how to engage with analytical output in ways that produce genuine insight rather than false confidence.

This matters because your AI buddies are extraordinarily good at analysis.

They can process data at scales humans cannot match and identify patterns invisible to human perception. They can run calculations, test scenarios, and generate insights faster than any individual or team. The analytical capabilities of these systems are genuinely impressive.

But analysis doesn't interpret itself.

When you prompt Claude, it can confirm when two variables are correlated. It cannot tell you whether that correlation is meaningful. It can identify a pattern in data. It cannot tell you whether the pattern reflects reality or an artifact of how the data was collected. It can generate a conclusion with high confidence. It cannot tell you whether that confidence is warranted.

That is, unless you ask it to and then carefully vet the source material.

***

Have you noticed that the media will refer to "AI" as if it's *Rosie the Robot* from *The Jetsons*? Remember the helpful autonomous assistant that worked independently and only needed occasional direction?

Most people talk about AI like it's Rosie the Robot
from *The Jetsons* — a helpful autonomous assistant
that works independently and just needs occasional direction.

Rosie the Robot is a fictional character from *The Jetsons*, originally produced by Hanna-Barbera. All rights to the character are held by their respective owners. This illustration is an original work and constitutes a descriptive cultural reference under fair use. No endorsement or affiliation is implied.

And, in doing so, this misunderstands the fundamental architecture of how we interact with these systems.

The Large Language Models that power conversational AI: GPT, Claude, Gemini, are not autonomous agents. They are prediction engines trained on patterns in human text. They have no goals, no preferences, no conception of *"better"* or *"worse"* beyond statistical likelihood. Every response is a probability distribution across possible next tokens, shaped entirely by the context window you provide: your prompt, the conversation history, the implicit framing in how you ask.

Intelligence emerges not from the model alone, but from the interaction design between human and system. How you frame a question determines which regions of the model's latent space get activated. Which outputs you accept or reject creates an implicit training signal for your own collaboration pattern. How you interpret results determines whether you're extracting genuine insight or sophisticated-sounding nonsense.

There are other configurations—agentic systems with tool use, memory, and goal-directed behavior—that operate with genuine autonomy. Those raise different questions about control and alignment. But this book addresses something more immediate: the 95% of AI interaction that happens through a chat interface, where outcomes depend less on the model's capabilities than on the sophistication of the thinking brought to it.

KEY INSIGHT: *Analysis Does Not Interpret Itself*

When working with your AI tool, it can identify that two variables correlate at r=0.73, but you must decide whether that relationship is causal, coincidental, or confounded.

Yes, your AI tool can surface a pattern in customer behavior, but you must determine whether you're seeing a genuine trend or sampling bias. And, yes, it can generate conclusions with numerical precision to three decimal places, but you must evaluate whether that precision reflects actual certainty or merely computational confidence.

The model has no epistemological framework. It cannot distinguish between correlation and causation, between pattern and noise, between what is true and what is merely consistent with its training data. Human judgment remains essential, serving as the interpretive layer that transforms statistical output into actionable insight.

High Analytical Partnership is evident when you engage with AI analysis the way Hume engaged with knowledge: actively, skeptically, and productively. Maintaining the creative tension between computational power and human discernment.

Interact with AI like Hume? What does this look like in practice?

You ask: *"what would falsify about this?"* before accepting the analytical output.

You prompt your AI tool for a market analysis predicting 23% growth. High Analytical Partnership interrogates the method:

"What data was this trained on? What structural assumptions are embedded in the analysis? What leading indicators would signal this forecast is wrong? What does the confidence interval mean here?"

Then, you prompt again for disconfirmation. You ask your AI tool to steelman the bearish case, to identify the weakest assumptions and to surface what's missing from the analysis.

The result is either an analysis that survives adversarial questioning and can be trusted proportionally, or one that reveals its brittleness. Both outcomes are valuable. What you avoid is false precision: believing a forecast because it sounds authoritative rather than because it has been tested against reality.

Are you able to distinguish between precision and accuracy?

Hint: Consider what the model is confident about and what you should be confident about.

KEY INSIGHT: *Wrong with Confidence*
Low Analytical Partnership produces a distinctive failure mode: being precisely wrong rather than approximately right.

You prompt, the model produces a sophisticated analysis with supporting data, and you proceed without subjecting it to adversarial questioning. The recommendation gets adopted and the projection gets budgeted. The conclusion drives strategy. Then reality diverges consistently, and the gap between predicted and actual compounds over time.

The pattern becomes recognizable: analyses that seem rigorous in the moment but don't hold up to implementation. Forecasts that are precise but systematically biased. Recommendations that address the question as framed but miss the actual problem.

Do your AI-assisted analyses look impressive in PowerPoint but underperform in practice? Are your projections confident but consistently off in the same direction? Do you find yourself working with increasingly sophisticated tools while producing outputs that fail to map cleanly to operational reality?

This reflects a problem with the partnership structure.

The model can generate analysis at superhuman speed and scale. But it cannot evaluate its own epistemological foundations. It cannot recognize when it's operating outside its training distribution. It cannot tell you when confidence should be withheld.

David Hume accepted claims only after rigorous interrogation. He understood that sound thinking requires active questioning and earned his conclusions through systematic doubt.

The same principle applies to every output your AI generates. Trust it proportionally to how thoroughly you've tested it.

Chapter 8: Synthesis Capability
—Sen no Rikyū

In sixteenth-century Japan, tea was never just tea. The warlords who commanded armies and controlled provinces collected Chinese ceramics with the intensity Renaissance princes brought to commissioning Michelangelo. A single Song dynasty tea bowl, with its perfect celadon glaze, could cost more than a minor lord's annual rice yield. These gatherings were political performances dressed in ritual. When you received an invitation, you understood the message: you mattered in the hierarchy of power. When you hosted, you demonstrated exactly where you stood.

The tea ceremony itself, *chanoyu*, had existed in various forms since the ninth century, when Buddhist monks first carried tea seeds from China's mountains to Japan's monasteries. Over seven centuries, the practice evolved across East Asia. In China's Tang Dynasty (618-907 CE), monks ground tea leaves into fine powder and whisked it with hot water, a method that traveled to Japan along with Zen Buddhism. By the Muromachi period (1336-1573), Japanese aristocrats had developed elaborate rituals around tea. These ceremonies emphasized what Japan had learned to value from eight centuries of looking toward China as the pinnacle of civilization: perfection, symmetry, mathematical precision in beauty.

Then came a merchant's son from Sakai who changed everything.

Sen no Rikyū was born in 1522 into a family of fish wholesalers in Sakai, a prosperous port city where trade created fortunes outside the traditional aristocratic channels. He studied tea under masters who served the ruling class. By his thirties, he was teaching tea to Oda Nobunaga, the warlord who would nearly unify Japan. After Nobunaga's assassination, Rikyū became tea master to Toyotomi Hideyoshi, the peasant general who completed the unification and became the most powerful man in the country.

Over four decades, Rikyū did something more profound than master an existing art. He saw connections others had missed. He recognized that elements from completely different traditions, each with its own history and logic, could fuse into something that had never existed before.

Sen no Rikyū (1522 - 1591) Hasegawa Tōhaku

What Rikyū synthesized were traditions that had developed separately over centuries, each with its own practitioners, its own assumptions about what mattered.

Zen Buddhism had arrived in Japan during the twelfth century, carried by monks who had studied in Chinese monasteries. These monks brought meditation practices that emphasized direct experience over intellectual understanding. A Zen master might spend thirty years teaching students to sit in silence, to watch their thoughts arise and dissolve, to recognize that the boundary between self and world was less solid than it appeared.

The practice was austere. Monks rose before dawn, sat for hours, worked in gardens, and ate simple food. The teaching was that ordinary activities, performed with complete attention, could become pathways to enlightenment. Sweeping a floor could be meditation. Preparing a meal could be practice. But this remained a monastic path. Zen offered no framework for social gatherings among the powerful, no aesthetic vocabulary for material objects.

Chinese culture had shaped Japanese aspiration for eight centuries. Poetry, calligraphy, painting, ceramics, the entire vocabulary of refinement came from China. When a Japanese aristocrat wanted to demonstrate sophistication, he displayed Chinese objects. When craftsmen wanted to achieve mastery, they attempted to replicate Chinese techniques. The aesthetic philosophy that came with these objects emphasized transcendence of human limitation. A perfect glaze showed no trace of the hand that made it. A symmetrical form achieved mathematical purity. The goal was to eliminate accidents, to remove the marks of making, to create something that approached the eternal.

Japanese potters working in village kilns like Bizen and Shigaraki produced vessels that bore the signatures of their making. Wood-fired kilns deposited ash on clay surfaces. Iron-rich local clay emerged from firing mottled and irregular. Glazes cracked as they cooled, creating networks of fine lines. These effects were unpredictable, unrepeatable, evidence of process rather than perfection. For centuries, such vessels were considered inferior to Chinese imports. They were functional, perhaps charming in their rustic directness, but certainly unsuitable for important occasions.

Shigaraki stoneware jar. Muromachi period, early 15th century.

Architecture followed its own traditions. Japanese buildings used wood, paper, and woven grass mats. They opened gardens and created spaces that acknowledged seasons that allowed weather to be felt. But tea rooms, when aristocrats built them, imitated Chinese formal halls. They were large, decorated, designed to impress through scale and ornament.

Social ritual was governed by codes that defined every interaction. Samurai culture prescribed precise behaviors for how inferiors approached superiors, how guests entered homes, how meals were served. These hierarchies were encoded in language itself. The words you used to address someone changed based on their rank relative to yours. Space reinforced these distinctions. In a formal gathering, where you sat determined where you stood.

All of these elements existed. None of them suggested the others. A Zen monk meditating in a temple was not thinking about tea bowls. A potter in Bizen was not thinking about social hierarchy. A craftsman building a tea room was not thinking about Buddhist philosophy. The elements were separate, each with its own internal coherence.

Rikyū's insight was architectural in the deepest sense. He saw that Zen presence could transform a social gathering from performance into shared experience. If the point was not to display status but to inhabit the present moment together, then everything about the ceremony would change.

He recognized that the accidents Japanese potters tried to minimize could become the very source of beauty. A crack in a glaze told the story of fire and cooling, of materials responding to heat. The asymmetry of a hand-formed bowl showed human touch. The patina that developed over years of use testified to an object's participation in life. These were not flaws to overcome but qualities to value. They made objects more honest, more particular, more themselves.

He understood that small spaces created possibilities that grand rooms could not. When you forced professionals into physical proximity, when you made the entrance so low that even a warlord had to bow and crawl through, you created conditions for a different kind of interaction. The room itself could dissolve the hierarchies that normally structured every social moment.

But Rikyū understood something more sophisticated than simply prefer simplicity to ostentation or imperfection to perfection. He recognized that these seemingly separate insights belonged to the same philosophical framework. Zen presence, Japanese craft, architectural intimacy, and a reimagining of Chinese aesthetics all expressed variations of a single underlying truth.

Rikyū gave this truth a name: *wabi-sabi.*

The term itself combines two words that had existed in Japanese poetry for centuries. *Wabi* originally described the loneliness of living apart from society, the poverty of a hermit's existence. *Sabi* meant the beauty of aging and weathering, the patina that time leaves on objects and landscapes. In earlier poetry, these were melancholy concepts, tinged with loss. Rikyū transformed them into a unified aesthetic philosophy, then fused that philosophy with Zen practice and Japanese craft traditions.

Wabi-sabi is difficult to translate precisely because it names something that had no name before Rikyū articulated it. At its core, it recognizes that imperfection, impermanence, and incompleteness are not deficiencies but the very conditions of beauty. The weathered wood shows its history. The cracked bowl reveals its making. The single flower in its simplicity acknowledges that it will fade. Nothing lasts. Nothing is finished. Nothing achieves perfection. And these truths, rather than being disappointments, are what make beauty possible and meaningful.

Designed and implemented by MAKHNO Studio. Photo rights: MAKHNO Studio. Creative Commons license may be used free of charge. Photo Credit: Serhii Kadulin.

KEY INSIGHT: *True Synthesis Creates a New Way of Seeing*
Rikyū took Zen mindfulness, Japanese craft traditions, architectural intimacy, and Chinese aesthetics reimagined through a different lens. He fused them into *wabi-sabi*, a philosophy that had never existed before.

Once you understood this framework, you could not *unsee* it. It became a way of perceiving everything. True synthesis does more than combine elements. It creates an entirely new way of seeing that makes the separate pieces finally make sense together.

Every choice in Rikyū's tea ceremony became an expression of *wabi-sabi* made tangible.

Consider the tea bowls. Instead of Chinese porcelain with its perfect glazes, Rikyū chose rough Japanese vessels from village kilns. A Raku bowl, created through a firing technique Rikyū helped develop, felt warm in your hands. Its thick walls held heat. Its irregular surface created specific points of contact between clay and skin. The glaze might crack during cooling, creating fine networks of lines. These cracks were called *kannyu*, and they were valued, not hidden. As tea stained these cracks over years of use, the bowl developed its own unrepeatable pattern, a visual record of its particular history.

A Bizen bowl, fired in an anagama kiln for days, emerged covered in ash deposits. The ash melted in the intense heat, creating natural glazes in tones of rust and amber. No two pieces emerged the same. The potter could guide the process but could not control it completely. The fire collaborated in the making.

A Shigaraki bowl, formed from iron-rich local clay, might show scorch marks where it stood closest to the flames. These marks, called *kogeyaki*, testified to the bowl's journey through fire. What Chinese aesthetics would have considered a flaw, Rikyū's philosophy transformed into evidence of authenticity.

The flowers arranged for the tea ceremony, *chabana*, were equally deliberate in their simplicity. A single branch of cherry blossoms in early spring. A camellia stem in winter. A morning glory that would last only hours. These arrangements acknowledged impermanence. The flowers were allowed to show their natural form, including asymmetry, including the way stems curved or leaves turned. The containers were often simple bamboo or unglazed ceramic. The aesthetic rejected the elaborate flower arrangements, *rikka*, used in formal settings, which demonstrated technical virtuosity and created permanent-seeming sculptures. Rikyū's flowers were alive, temporary, real.

Chabana design by Ric Bansho Carrasco in a Shoshin Pottery chabana pot created in Guang Ming Temple. Creative Commons (2026).

The tea room itself embodied every principle of the philosophy. Rikyū's most famous room, the Taian, still exists in Kyoto. It measures only two tatami mats, roughly six feet by six feet. This is smaller than most professionals's closets. The ceiling height varies, creating intimacy. The entrance, the *nijiriguchi*, is two feet high. You cannot walk through it. You must remove your sword if you carry one, set aside your status, and crawl through on hands and knees. Inside, you sit on the floor with others, shoulder to shoulder.

The walls are made from clay mixed with straw, their texture visible and irregular. No attempt is made to create a smooth surface. The *tokonoma* alcove holds a single scroll and the flower arrangement. Light enters through shoji screens covered in translucent paper, creating soft illumination without harsh shadows. Every surface invites touch. The wooden post in the corner might show its bark. The bamboo ceiling reveals individual stalks bound with natural fiber.

Color is muted. Earth tones predominate, the browns and grays and russets of natural materials. The aesthetic is one of restraint carried to its logical conclusion. But this restraint does not feel austere. It feels intimate, concentrated, intentional. Every element serves the whole. Nothing extra remains.

> **KEY INSIGHT:** *Integration Feels Inevitable in Retrospect*
>
> Rikyū made the tea room small and the entrance low. He stripped away decoration and used rough Japanese bowls instead of perfect Chinese ones, these choices were radical and violated every convention at the time. Once made, they seemed obvious.

This is the key to genuine synthesis. The integration feels inevitable in retrospect, as if the elements always belonged together and simply needed someone to recognize how they fit.

The End and What Survived

Rikyū's influence extended far beyond tea. Japanese architecture, garden design, flower arrangement, ceramics, calligraphy, even the plating of food in kaiseki cuisine were all transformed by *wabi-sabi*. The philosophy he articulated became foundational to Japanese aesthetics, shaping how artists and craftsmen approached their work across generations.

By 1591, Rikyū was sixty-nine. He had served Toyotomi Hideyoshi for nearly two decades. He was the most influential aesthetic arbiter in Japan. His judgment on a tea bowl could determine its value. His approval of a tea room design could establish a reputation. His students included some of the most powerful professionals in the country.

Then Hideyoshi ordered him to commit ritual suicide.

The reasons remain debated by historians. Some sources suggest Rikyū had offended Hideyoshi by placing a statue of himself above the gate of a temple, forcing those who passed beneath to show obeisance to the tea master. Others speculate that Rikyū's aesthetic philosophy, with its emphasis on simplicity and restraint, had become an implicit criticism of Hideyoshi's increasingly grandiose displays of power. The warlord was building a tea room with walls covered in gold. He was staging tea gatherings for hundreds. Rikyū's philosophy suggested that such displays missed the entire point.

Perhaps it was simply the risk of being too close to absolute power, of becoming too influential, of having aesthetic judgments carry more weight than a merchant's son should be allowed to command.

On the designated day, Rikyū invited his closest students for a final tea ceremony. He gave away his implements. He gave his favorite tea bowl to a student who had admired it. Then he entered a small room, composed a death poem, and ended his life according to the samurai code that governed such things, though he was not a samurai by birth.

Hideyoshi outlived him by only seven years. When Hideyoshi died in 1598, his empire began to fracture. Within fifteen years, the Tokugawa clan would seize power and establish a shogunate that would last two and a half centuries.

Rikyū's synthesis endured. His descendants, the Sen family, continued teaching tea ceremony. The schools they established still exist. His tea rooms remain preserved as cultural treasures. His aesthetic vocabulary spread throughout Japanese culture and eventually across the world. Today, five centuries later, millions practice the tea ceremony in traditions that trace directly back to Rikyū.

The term *wabi-sabi* is recognized globally. Contemporary designers and artists invoke it. The philosophy proved more durable than political power.

Synthesis Capability is the fourth dimension of AIQ.

This dimension measures your ability to integrate diverse outputs from your AI collaborations into coherent frameworks, to recognize what belongs together, to resolve contradictions, and to create unified understanding from separate insights.

This capability matters because AI tools produce outputs in response to individual prompts. When you work with Claude, ChatGPT or any other AI system, each conversation exists independently unless you deliberately connect them. The tools themselves have no memory across sessions, no ability to see how yesterday's analysis relates to today's strategy document, no sense of an accumulating whole.

That sense of the whole is human work. It lives in your ability to recognize patterns across separate interactions, to remember what the tool generated last week and how it connects to what you are exploring now.

Not too long ago I was on a call with Mike Krieger, Chief Product Officer of Anthropic, and he jokingly described Claude as *"the world's most intelligent amnesiac."*

I laughed aloud because I knew exactly what he meant by that.

Mike was pointing to something fundamental about how these systems work. Each conversation starts fresh. There's no persistent memory that carries forward automatically. No matter how brilliant the last conversation was, the next one begins with a blank slate. That is, unless you deliberately bring context forward.

Mike also mentioned, as a funny side observation, that Claude *"really likes the Golden Gate Bridge."* This caught my attention. Could an AI system that starts fresh each time actually have preferences?

"I don't have preferences," the AI says. "But this bridge keeps coming up."

So I tested it.

"What do you think about the Golden Gate Bridge?" I asked.

Claude gave me an incredibly upbeat response about engineering elegance, the international orange color against fog, Art Deco towers, how the bridge anchors that specific geography. It sounded like appreciation. It read like preference.

Here's what matters: Claude does not have opinions that persist. Those preferences we think we have discovered are patterns in training data, not actual memory. Every conversation starts fresh. The thoughtfulness is real but the persistence is not.

This is not a bug to be fixed. It's a fundamental characteristic of how these systems work.

And it reveals something critical about refined AIQ: the tools may remember facts; you remember meaning.

Advanced tools now offer persistent memory within defined workspaces. They can recall past conversations, access shared documents, maintain context across sessions. But even with these capabilities, the tool cannot independently decide what's relevant. It cannot determine what should be carried forward. It cannot know how today's work connects to your larger vision.

It responds to what you invoke, not what it independently recalls.

That capacity to see across separate outputs, to recognize unity among fragments, to construct something larger from individual pieces, to know what matters and what to discard—this belongs entirely to you.

You are the architect who envisions the cathedral while the tool sees individual stones. The tool may access past conversations; you understand which past insights should shape present decisions.

This is a fundamental asymmetry to leverage. The tool's fresh perspective can challenge your assumptions. Your continuity of vision gives coherence to the tool's outputs.

The question is not whether the tool remembers. The question is whether you are directing what should be remembered and why.

KEY INSIGHT: *You Are the Thread of Continuity*

When you work with AI tools, each conversation starts fresh unless you bring forward what came before.

This is a fundamental asymmetry to leverage. The tool's fresh perspective can challenge your assumptions. Your continuity of vision can give coherence to the tool's outputs. The question is not whether the tool remembers, but whether *you* are directing what should be remembered and why.

Ask your AI tool to analyze a market opportunity, and it will provide analysis. Ask it to generate strategic options, and it will generate options. Request research, creative alternatives, different perspectives, and the tool will deliver all of these, often brilliantly. But it cannot integrate them for you. It cannot tell you which analysis connects to which strategy, which research findings contradict which assumptions, how the pieces might fit together into something coherent.

Each output stands alone. Each prompt produces its own response. The connections between outputs, the ways they might reinforce or contradict or combine into something larger, remain invisible to the tool. You must see those connections. You must do the integration.

High Synthesis Capability occurs when you recognize when two separate outputs from different sessions are actually expressing the same insight from different angles. It entails noticing when outputs contradict each other and then deciding which contradiction reveals something true about the complexity of the situation versus which one reveals an error in your prompting. It unfolds when you build cumulative understanding across many interactions, so that each new output adds to a structure you are constructing over time.

Low Synthesis Capability treats each AI interaction as isolated. You prompt, receive output, use it, and move on. The next interaction starts fresh. Nothing accumulates. The work the tool produces remains fragmented because you never integrate it. You have many pieces. You have no whole.

How to Recognize High Synthesis Capability

An individual with high Synthesis Capability *builds* across sessions. They treat interactions with AI tools as contributions to an ongoing project, not as independent transactions. What they learned in one conversation informs how they frame the next question. Insights accumulate. Frameworks develop. Over weeks and months, they are constructing something that exceeds what any single session could produce.

You can see this in *how* they work. They keep notes on what patterns emerged in previous analyses. When they start a new session, they might say to the tool, *"In our previous conversation, you identified three constraints. I want to explore the second one further."* They reference earlier outputs. They build on them. Each session adds a layer to what came before.

They recognize when separate outputs point to the same underlying truth. Imagine someone exploring a business decision. They ask their AI tool to analyze the market from three different angles. Someone with low Synthesis Capability treats these as three options to choose among.

With High Synthesis Capability, you read all three analyses and recognize that each one, despite using different frameworks, keeps highlighting the same constraint. That constraint, visible only when the outputs are seen together, becomes the actual insight. The three analyses were not offering different perspectives. They were revealing the same truth through different lenses.

Someone with high Synthesis Capability treats contradictions as information. What assumptions differ between these outputs? Under what conditions is each recommendation correct? What does the contradiction reveal about the actual complexity of the situation? The contradiction becomes the thing to understand, not an inconvenience to eliminate.

You create coherence where none existed.

This represents the highest level of Synthesis Capability. You are not simply organizing separate insights. You are finding the underlying principle that unifies them, the deeper logic that explains why these seemingly disparate outputs belong together. Like Rikyū recognizing that imperfection, simplicity, and presence all expressed variations of the same philosophy even though they came from different cultural traditions. You are discovering the framework that makes the separate pieces finally make sense as parts of a whole.

And you recognize the difference between synthesis and aggregation. Aggregation is easy. You can gather many outputs from AI tools, assemble them into a document, label it *"comprehensive analysis,"* and feel productive. But if the outputs remain separate, if each stands alone rather than connecting to the others, you have collected but not synthesized.

Synthesis means the outputs have become parts of a whole. Each one makes more sense in the context of the others. The structure you have built reveals something that was invisible when the pieces were separate. You have created integration, not just accumulated volume.

Rikyū's tea room includes only what serves the unified vision. The single scroll in the *tokonoma* alcove. The seasonal flower. The rough bowl. Each element is present because it expresses *wabi-sabi*. Each element makes the others more meaningful. The tea room achieves synthesis through exclusion as much as through what it contains.

This is synthesis at its most sophisticated.

Neither comprehensive coverage of every possible element, nor multiple perspectives included for the sake of completeness. But selective integration toward a coherent whole. The question for your own work is whether you are doing similar integration in your collaborations with AI tools, at whatever scale your work requires.

Key Insight : *Your Work Product Is Not Sacred.* You can generate endless outputs and ask your AI tool for ten different strategic approaches before breakfast. And so can everyone else.

You produce more content in a single afternoon than your grandfather produced in an entire year. And so can everyone else.

Whatever you're producing, be it the report, strategy deck, market analysis, or creative brief, it's no longer precious. The work product that used to take you weeks and demonstrate your expertise?

Someone with high AIQ generated it this morning. Before you finished your second meeting.

Sen no Rikyū spent years perfecting the tea ceremony. Every element carefully chosen, every gesture deliberate, every object placed with intention. The rough tea bowl, the bare room, the specific guest—all of it synthesized into a particular kind of meaning. It was art. It was irreplaceable and it took a lifetime to master.

"You produce more content in a single afternoon than your grandfather produced in an entire year."

Consider this: the most influential work Sen no Rikyū' produced came to fruition between around 1570 and 1591, the two decades he served as tea master to Japan's most powerful warlords—first Oda Nobunaga, then Toyotomi Hideyoshi.

Nearly five hundred years separate Rikyū's tea room from your inbox.

In Rikyū's lifetime, information traveled at the speed of a horse or a sailing vessel. A letter from Sakai to Kyoto, which are roughly fifty miles apart, took one full day by courier. The total volume of written material a person of Rikyū's stature might encounter in a year could be measured in dozens of scrolls and letters. The Buddhist texts he studied, poetry he read, and political correspondence he received could all fit in a single room. His inputs were limited, and he had decades to integrate them into a unified philosophy.

The world you inhabit bears no resemblance to this.

Rikyū had limited inputs and unlimited time to integrate them. You have unlimited inputs and no time to integrate anything.

Once again, because this is really important: your work product is no longer sacred. The synthesis, which you contribute, is. Anyone can generate the fragments now. But what they can't do, what most professionals are failing catastrophically to do, is integrate those fragments into something coherent; into something that truly answers the question or use to make a decision.

High Synthesis Capability means you can produce in minutes what used to take weeks. But more importantly, it means you can look at everything coming at you, the AI outputs, the messages, the notifications, the summaries, and extract what matters. You can see across the fragments, build the whole and find the signal while everyone else is drowning in noise.

That capacity: to integrate rather than just accumulate is the only moat left. The outputs are abundant and synthesis is scarce.

That is where your leverage lives.

Chapter 9: Iterative Refinement — Lise Meitner

I n December 1938, Elise *"Lise"* Meitner received a letter that would change the course of history. Meitner was living in Sweden, alone, having fled Nazi Germany just five months earlier. For thirty years, she had been one of the leading physicists at the Kaiser Wilhelm Institute in Berlin, working in a laboratory she had helped build, collaborating with chemist Otto Hahn on experiments that were pushing the boundaries of nuclear physics. But as an Austrian Jew, her protection under Austrian citizenship vanished the moment Germany annexed Austria in March 1938. Colleagues who had worked beside her for decades now looked away in hallways. The university that had barely tolerated her presence as a woman now found her unacceptable as a Jew.

Meitner left Berlin in July with ten marks in her purse, the limit of what Jews were allowed to carry. A colleague, the Dutch chemist Dirk Coster, had hidden a diamond ring in her coat pocket as she boarded the train—something valuable she could sell or use to bribe a border guard if necessary. Meitner crossed into Holland at night, terrified the guards would turn her back but they let her through.

Now, at sixty years old, Meitner was starting over in Stockholm. She had a makeshift position at a university where she knew almost no one. Her Swedish was poor. The laboratory facilities were inadequate. She was separated from the Berlin lab that held thirty years of her work, from the equipment she knew intimately, from the collaboration with Hahn that had produced some of the most important nuclear physics research of the era.

The letter from Hahn was brief and puzzled, almost apologetic. An experiment had produced results that made no sense to him, and he wanted her opinion.

For several years, scientists across Europe had been bombarding uranium atoms with neutrons, trying to create elements heavier than uranium. The expectation was straightforward: uranium had ninety-two protons in its nucleus. Add neutrons, and perhaps some of them would decay into protons, creating element ninety-three, ninety-four, or even heavier. This was the established thinking. This was what the physics predicted.

But Hahn's latest experiments showed something impossible. When he bombarded uranium with neutrons and then analyzed the resulting materials through careful chemical separation, he found barium. Barium has only fifty-six protons, roughly half the number in uranium. It was as if the uranium nucleus had split in two.

Hahn was one of the finest chemists in Europe. He knew his chemical analysis was right. He had identified barium definitively using techniques he had refined over decades. But he could not explain how barium could appear from uranium. It violated every model of atomic structure he knew. Nuclei could chip off small particles, alpha rays or beta rays. They could absorb neutrons. But split completely in half? That seemed physically absurd.

Lise Meitner (1878–1968), Austrian-Swedish physicist who helped explain nuclear fission in 1938–39.

Hahn wrote to Meitner almost apologetically. Perhaps there was contamination in his samples. Perhaps he had made an error somewhere in his procedure. Could she help him understand what was happening?

Meitner did not dismiss the results. She did not assume error. Instead, she took the data seriously and began to work through what it might mean.

The Process of Refinement

What happened over the next few weeks was a systematic refinement of understanding in response to evidence.

Meitner had been thinking about nuclear structure for three decades. She had developed mental models of how the nucleus worked, tested those models against experimental results, adjusted them as new data emerged. She understood nuclear physics as well as anyone alive. But this data from Hahn contradicted her models. It contradicted everyone's models.

Meitner could have done what many scientists do when faced with contradictory evidence: explained it away. The data must be wrong. There must be contamination. The technique must have introduced artifacts. These are reasonable responses when established theory meets anomalous results.

Instead, Meitner began adjusting her understanding.

She was spending Christmas in the small Swedish village of Kungälv with her nephew, Otto Frisch, who was himself a physicist working in Copenhagen. On walks through the snow, Frisch on skis, Meitner on foot despite the December cold and they talked through the problem.

What if the uranium nucleus was not as stable as everyone assumed? The prevailing model treated the nucleus like a solid ball, held together by forces that made it essentially permanent. But there was another model, less popular, that compared the nucleus to a liquid drop. In that model, the nucleus could deform, oscillate, and stretch.

If you thought of the nucleus as a liquid drop, what would happen when you added neutrons? The drop would become larger, more unstable. It might oscillate. And if it oscillated violently enough, it might stretch into a dumbbell shape. At some point, the electrical repulsion between all those positively charged protons would overcome the nuclear force holding the nucleus together, and the dumbbell would pinch apart into two smaller drops.

This was not completely new thinking. The liquid drop model had been proposed years earlier by George Gamow and developed further by Niels Bohr. But it had been theoretical. No one had observed it happening.

Meitner worked through the physics carefully. If a uranium nucleus split into two fragments of roughly equal size, those fragments would fly apart. They would repel each other electrically because both would have positive charge. That repulsion would release energy. How much energy?

She calculated it in her head during that walk, using Einstein's equation relating mass to energy. As you recall, Einstein's equation is:

$$E = mc^2$$

Where:

- E = energy
- m = mass
- c = speed of light in a vacuum (approximately 300,000,000 meters per second, or 3×10^8 m/s)

The equation shows that mass and energy are interchangeable - a small amount of mass can be converted into an enormous amount of energy because the speed of light squared (c^2) is such a large number.

In the context of Meitner and Frisch's discovery, they used this equation to calculate that when a uranium nucleus split, the two daughter nuclei together had slightly less mass than the original uranium nucleus - and that *"missing"* mass was converted into about 200 million electron volts (200 MeV) of energy.

This explained where the explosive energy of nuclear fission came from.

The mass of uranium was known. The masses of the fragments would be slightly less than the original uranium nucleus. That missing mass would convert to energy. The amount of energy released by splitting a single uranium atom would be roughly two hundred million electron volts.

This was an enormous amount of energy from a single atom, roughly ten times more than any known radioactive decay. But the numbers worked. If the nucleus split, the energy release matched what Einstein's equation predicted.

By the end of the walk, they had the explanation. Uranium nuclei were splitting apart when bombarded with neutrons. This was nuclear fission, though they had not yet coined that term. Frisch suggested it a few weeks later, borrowing from the biological term for cell division.

> **KEY INSIGHT:** *Systematic Adjustment Over Sudden Revelation*
> Meitner refined her way to understanding through systematic adjustment. The anomalous data had been visible for years. Other scientists saw similar results and explained them away, trying to force the evidence into existing models or assuming error when it would not fit.

Meitner was different. She took the data seriously, asked what would have to be true for it to make sense, then adjusted her mental models incrementally and tested which parts could bend and which could not until model and data aligned.

Thirty Years of Preparation

What made Meitner's refinement possible was her thirty years of working directly with radioactive materials. She handled the substances, observed their behavior and learned their patterns. Meitner developed what you might refer to as empirical intuition: a deeply embodied sense of what uranium could and could not do, built from thousands of hours at the bench.

Meitner had started working with radioactivity in 1907, when the field was barely six years old. She was twenty-nine, one of the first women in Germany to earn a doctorate in physics. For the next thirty years, she worked at the *Kaiser Wilhelm Institute*, initially without salary because women could not hold official positions. She worked in a converted carpenter's shop in the basement because she was not allowed in the main laboratories where male students worked.

Meitner's collaboration with Otto Hahn began in those early years. Hahn was a chemist. Meitner was a physicist. Together, they investigated radioactive elements, discovering several new isotopes, developing techniques for separating and identifying radioactive materials. The collaboration was remarkably productive. By the 1930s, they were among the leading researchers in nuclear physics.

Otto Hahn (1879 - 1968). Known for: Discovery of radioactive elements (1905–1938), Radiothorium (228Th, 1905), Radioactinium (227Th, 1906), Mesothorium (228Ra, 1907), Ionium (230Th, 1907), Radioactive recoil (1909), Fajans–Paneth–Hahn Law, Protactinium (Pa, 1917), Nuclear isomerism (1921), Applied Radiochemistry (1936), Rubidium-strontium dating (1938), Discovery of nuclear fission (1938). **Awards:** Nobel Prize in Chemistry (1944), Max Planck Medal (1949), Pour le Mérite (1952), Faraday Lectureship Prize (1956), Wilhelm Exner Medal (1958), Legion of Honour (1959), Enrico Fermi Award (1966)

Throughout this period, Meitner was constantly refining her understanding. Each experiment revealed something. Each anomaly required explanation. Some results confirmed expectations. Others contradicted them, forcing adjustment. Her mental model of the nucleus grew more sophisticated, more nuanced, more accurate with each iteration.

Meitner was not starting from scratch in December 1938. She was applying a method she had developed over thirty years: take data seriously, question models when they conflict with evidence, adjust understanding systematically, test adjustments against new experiments.

The fission discovery was this method operating at its highest level. Decades of iterative refinement had prepared her to see what others missed.

> **KEY INSIGHT:** *Each Iteration Builds Understanding Over Time*
> This is the essence of iterative refinement: systematically adjusting understanding in response to evidence until model and reality align.

Meitner had been putting this into practice her entire career. Each experiment refined her thinking. Each anomaly prompted recalibration. Over thirty years, this process made her one of the world's foremost nuclear physicists and prepared her to recognize fission when the evidence finally became undeniable.

Recognition and Injustice

In January 1939, Meitner and Frisch published their theoretical explanation of fission in the journal *Nature*. A few days later, Hahn and his assistant Fritz Strassmann published the experimental evidence in *Naturwissenschaften*. The physics community immediately recognized the significance. Within months, laboratories around the world were confirming the results and exploring the implications.

The work led directly to the development of nuclear weapons and nuclear power. Meitner refused to participate in weapons research, though she was invited. When someone later referred to her as the "mother of the atomic bomb," she replied firmly that she had nothing to do with the bomb.

In 1944, the Nobel Prize in Chemistry was awarded to Otto Hahn alone for the discovery of nuclear fission. Meitner was not included.

The exclusion was noted immediately as an injustice. Albert Einstein referred to Meitner *"the German Marie Curie."* Colleagues who understood the physics knew that without Meitner's theoretical explanation, Hahn's chemical findings would have remained a puzzling anomaly, not a paradigm-shifting discovery. The Nobel committee later acknowledged the omission as one of the most significant errors in the prize's history.

The reasons were complicated. Meitner was in exile, which made communication difficult during wartime. The prize committee may have been biased against a woman, against a Jewish scientist, against someone working outside established institutions. Hahn himself believed Meitner deserved recognition, though he did not refuse the prize or publicly advocate for her inclusion at the time.

The prize announcement came in November 1945. Otto Hahn, still detained with other German nuclear scientists at Farm Hall—a country estate near Cambridge where the British had quietly installed listening devices—learned he'd won the Nobel Prize for Chemistry when a colleague showed him the notice in the Daily Telegraph. His fellow internees, reading the same carefully worded citation about "the discovery of the fission of heavy atomic nuclei," understood immediately what wasn't said: Lise Meitner's name appeared nowhere.

There was singing that evening at Farm Hall. Speeches, jokes, congratulations. The strange celebration of men who'd built their careers on radioactive elements, now themselves contained and monitored, uncertain whether their work had made them heroes or something else entirely.

Meitner, by then living in Stockholm, had known this moment was coming. She'd been nominated forty-nine times for Nobel Prizes in Physics and Chemistry over two decades. Colleagues who understood what had happened in December 1938—the experimental observation Hahn couldn't explain, the letter he'd sent her asking for *"some sort of fantastic explanation,"* the walk through the snow where she and Frisch worked out the physics that made sense of it all—had repeatedly put her name forward. The chemistry committee looked at these nominations and saw a physicist encroaching on chemical territory. The physics committee saw a theorist, not an experimentalist, and deferred to tradition.

Two years after the prize announcement, Hahn came to Stockholm for the delayed Nobel ceremony. Meitner met him at the train station. She assumed, and her colleagues had suggested, that Hahn would acknowledge her contribution in his acceptance speech.

Hahn did not.

When the Nobel Committee's sealed deliberations finally became public fifty years later, the pattern emerged clearly: interdisciplinary work assessed by professionals with disciplinary loyalties, a woman physicist evaluated by male chemists who didn't understand why physicists found her contribution essential, a Jewish refugee judged by Swedes who'd spent the war isolated from the international scientific community that recognized her centrality to the discovery. And running through the committee discussions, a presumption that would have been familiar to anyone who'd spent thirty years watching male collaborators receive solo credit for joint work: the assumption that Hahn's chemical identification of barium was the discovery, and Meitner's explanation of how uranium nuclei could split to produce barium was merely... clarification.

The physicist Jeremy Bernstein would later write that Hahn had discovered something without knowing what he'd discovered, similar to the astronomers who had detected noise in a radio telescope that turned out to be background radiation from the Big Bang. The observation mattered. But so did understanding what the observation meant.

Years later, in private correspondence, Meitner would describe that speech, that public erasing of three decades of partnership, as worse than the prize itself. Hahn had given her half the prize money and she donated it to help resettle Jewish refugee scientists. He had invited her to return to Berlin to head the physics department at what was now the Max Planck Institute and she declined. The recognition she wanted, the acknowledgment that mattered, never came.

The element meitnerium, atomic number 109, is named for her. Craters on the Moon and Venus bear her name. Meitner's contribution is now universally acknowledged in physics textbooks and histories of science. But she never received the Nobel Prize that her work merited.

What remains beyond dispute is her method. The systematic refinement that allowed her to interpret Hahn's puzzling data, that prepared her to recognize fission when others could not, that produced understanding from decades of careful iteration. This stands as a model for how genuine insight develops.

The pattern hasn't disappeared; it has accelerated.

Work goes unrecognized because it crosses boundaries that evaluators police rigidly. Because it's interpretive rather than procedural, collaborative rather than individually attributable, strategic rather than technical. Because the person who did it doesn't match the mental image of who does important work.

You've experienced some version of this. The insight you offered in a meeting that your manager repeated six months later as their own. The analysis you built that somehow became *"the team's work"* while your colleague's smaller contribution remained individually credited. The framework you developed dissolved into *"how we do things"* while the person who simply applied it got promoted. The pattern you identified that no one acknowledged until someone more senior said exactly the same thing.

AI makes this dynamic more treacherous, not less. The work product itself—the presentation, the report, the strategic document—can now be generated by anyone with access to the right tools. What remains valuable is exactly what Meitner provided: the interpretation, the synthesis, the judgment about what's happening and what it means. The invisible thinking that shapes the visible output.

This is the work most likely to be overlooked. Most easily attributed to whoever presents it. Hardest to defend when someone claims your contribution was merely *"helpful"* or *"collaborative."*

Meitner's story is more than historic fact. It's instruction. If you cannot make your invisible work visible, the pattern recognition AI cannot replicate, the systematic refinement that produces

breakthrough insight, the interpretive judgment that transforms observation into understanding, you will find yourself in her position. Essential to the outcome and absent from the credit, watching someone else accept recognition for work that would not exist without you.

The question is not whether this will happen. The question is whether you can develop capabilities so clear, so demonstrably valuable, so impossible to attribute to anyone else that even committees inclined toward dismissal cannot ignore what you've contributed.

That is about strategic necessity in a world where the outputs are abundant and the professionals who can interpret them remain rare.

Iterative Refinement is the fifth dimension of AIQ.

It measures your ability to systematically improve outputs from your AI tool through structured feedback, guiding work from initial draft to final form through progressive enhancement.

This capability matters because first outputs are rarely final outputs.

When you prompt your AI tool, you receive an initial response. That response reflects what the tool understood from your prompt, which may not perfectly match what you meant. It reflects patterns in the tool's training data, which may not serve your specific purpose. The output is raw material. Your judgment determines what happens next.

If you have low Iterative Refinement, you either accept the early output as is or abandon it entirely. You prompt, receive something approximating what you wanted, and use it without further development. Or, you receive something that misses the mark and start over with a completely new prompt, hoping this attempt will be better. Either way, there is no systematic improvement. Each attempt exists independently. Nothing compounds.

If you currently collaborate with your AI tools applying high Iterative Refinement, you treat the first output as the beginning of a conversation. You evaluate what works and what needs adjustment, providing specific feedback that produces measurable improvement. You enjoy building through iterations, with each one better than the last, until the final output meets the standard required.

KEY INSIGHT: *First Draft as Starting Point, Not Destination*
Low Iterative Refinement treats AI outputs as either acceptable or unacceptable. No systematic improvement happens. High Iterative Refinement understands the first output as the beginning of refinement.

Iterative Refinement in Practice

Consider the difference between vague and specific feedback. *"Make it better"* gives the tool nothing to work with. It will change something, but the change may not be an improvement. It might make the output different without making it better. *"The third paragraph loses focus—tighten the argument by removing the digression about quarterly earnings and instead develop the point about organizational structure"* is specific. The tool knows exactly what to adjust and why.

High Iterative Refinement gives specific feedback. It identifies precisely what is working and what needs change. It provides direction, not just judgment. Each iteration produces measurable progress toward the goal.

They know when to iterate and when to restart. Not everything can be refined efficiently. Sometimes the first output reveals that your initial prompt was fundamentally flawed. The direction is wrong, not just the execution. Someone with high Iterative Refinement recognizes when refinement would be inefficient, when starting fresh with a better-conceived prompt would produce better results faster than attempting to fix something structurally unsound.

They have a clear standard for completion. Someone with low Iterative Refinement either stops too early, settling for *"good enough,"* or continues too long, endlessly tinkering past the point of meaningful improvement. An individual with high Iterative Refinement recognizes quality for this particular task and stops when that standard is met. The goal is not perfection. The goal is meeting the requirement efficiently.

Their feedback becomes more precise with each iteration. The first round might be broad: *"This needs more concrete examples."*

The second becomes more specific: *"Replace the abstract explanation in paragraph two with a case study showing how a real company implemented this approach."*

The third is precise: *"Use the Crayola supply chain vertical integration as the case study—focus specifically on their decision to manufacture the color "green grass" using green grass from pastures in Grasse, France rather than continue sourcing from artificial turf suppliers."*

Each iteration narrows the gap between current state and target.

Most importantly, their iterations compound. Version two improves on version one. Version three improves on version two. The trajectory is clear. If you are generating variations without convergence, if version five is not measurably better than version three, you are cycling rather than refining.

You're working hard and have generated version after version. You've spent hours refining your prompts, and tried different approaches. You are iterating extensively.

When you step back and look at the pattern, you notice something unsettling: lateral movement rather than progress.

Version two is different from version one, but not better. Version five is not measurably closer to what you need than version three. You're trying. You're investing real effort. But somehow the effort isn't compounding. Each iteration expends energy without building toward your destination.

The Feedback Quality Gap

Why the Quality of Your Feedback Determines the Quality of Your AI Output

Based on Steiss, Tate, Graham et al. (2024), "Comparing the Quality of Human and ChatGPT Feedback of Students' Writing," *Learning and Instruction*, 91, University of California, Irvine, N = 198 essays.

> **Experienced educators with specialized feedback training outperformed AI in 4 of 5 feedback dimensions—not because they worked harder, but because their feedback was more diagnostically precise.**
>
> The difference between cycling through AI versions and compounding improvement is the same difference this research measured: **vague feedback produces variation; precise feedback produces progress.**

- Experienced Educators (15+ yrs, specialized training)
- ChatGPT (v3.5)

© ARQ Ninja (2026). All Rights Reserved

In 2024, researchers at the University of California, Irvine did something deceptively simple. They gathered 198 student essays and compared the feedback given by ChatGPT against feedback from experienced human educators. The educators had fifteen or more years in the classroom and specialized training in how to diagnose writing problems. The AI did not lose because it lacked knowledge or because it couldn't identify errors. It lost in four out of five feedback dimensions for a reason that may stop you cold: its feedback wasn't *diagnostically precise.*

The educators were not working harder nor were they spending more time. They were seeing something the AI couldn't see on its own — the specific structural failure, the exact moment where an argument lost its footing, the precise gap between what the writer intended and what landed on the page. And because they could name the problem with surgical accuracy, the path to improvement was clear.

This is the difference between cycling through AI versions and actually compounding improvement. Vague feedback produces variation. Precise feedback produces progress.

And here's what makes this personal: when you sit with an AI tool and iterate—when you go back and forth, refining a strategy document or a presentation or a critical email—you are the feedback mechanism. You are the one who has to diagnose what's wrong with what the AI just gave you. Not *"I don't like it."* Not *"try a different tone."* But *what specifically isn't working and why.*

Most folks have never been trained to do this. Why would they have been? Before AI, in modern use, the feedback loop was between you and your own thinking, or between you and a colleague who could ask clarifying questions. Now, you're directing an extraordinarily capable system that will follow your instructions to the letter, including your vague, misdirected ones. Your instructions are fixing one problem while quietly introducing many others.

The quality ceiling of everything AI produces for you is set right here, in this moment of feedback. It's by your ability to look at what came back and say, with precision, *this is what needs to change and this is why.*

Have you ever had this happen? You're in a rush. So, you react to what the AI tool produces without analyzing it carefully and sense something is wrong but can't quite articulate what specifically needs adjustment. You prompt again, hoping the tool will somehow intuit what you want.

"Make it more compelling." "Improve the flow." "Make it stronger."

The tool takes your vague direction and adjusts tone, adds adjectives, varies sentence structure—changes that feel different but don't address what's wrong. It can't read your mind. Without specific guidance about what to change and why, it generates variations, not improvements.

Sometimes the problem is persistence in the wrong direction.

You keep refining something that should be abandoned. You've invested effort—you don't want to waste it—so you continue polishing work that has fundamental problems. Maybe the entire structure is wrong or you're leading with product features when you should start with the customer problem. Maybe your analysis answers the wrong question.

The refinement is real. You're making the writing tighter, the data cleaner, the logic more coherent. But you're refining the wrong thing. Knowing when to abandon an approach and start fresh is as important as knowing how to refine.

Systematic Refinement

Lise Meitner's method was different. She refined relentlessly, but with precision.

When Otto Hahn wrote to her about finding barium in uranium experiments, a result that made no chemical sense, she did not respond with vague curiosity. She didn't iterate through random theoretical explanations hoping one would fit.

Instead, Meitner asked specific questions: *"What was the experimental procedure? How certain was the chemical identification? What other elements appeared? How much energy would be released if the nucleus split?"*

Each adjustment was based on evidence. With each iteration Meitner moved measurably closer to accurate understanding. When a model conflicted with data, she adjusted the model. And when the evidence demanded radical revision; recall when the experimental results for fission became undeniable, Meitner was willing to make that revision.

Decades of incremental refinement enabled her to develop mental flexibility in exactly the right way: confident in her foundations, willing to adjust when evidence required it.

Chapter 10: The Dimension You Don't See

There is a puzzle at the center of AI collaboration that is not being discussed enough. You sit down with ChatGPT to draft a strategy memo. The session feels productive. The AI generates coherent paragraphs and you refine them. The final document looks professional. The structure is clear, the language is confident and the examples are relevant. You feel satisfied with the work.

There is something that you cannot see: whether that memo is good. Not good relative to what you could have produced alone, but good relative to what someone with genuinely high AIQ would have produced using the same AI with the same raw materials. That comparison is invisible to you but the gap might be enormous. Or, it might not exist, except you have no reliable way to know.

This is not a matter of experience or effort. The problem is structural. And it begins with a cognitive illusion that AI amplifies dangerously.

When David Dunning and Justin Kruger conducted their now-famous study at Cornell in 1999, they discovered something unsettling about human self-assessment. They asked undergraduate students to complete tests of logical reasoning, grammar, and humor, then estimate their own performance. Students who scored in the bottom quartile, 12th percentile, estimated their performance at the 62nd percentile. They had overestimated by 50 percentile points.

The pattern revealed something deeper than simple overconfidence. Students who performed poorly lacked the metacognitive ability to recognize their poor performance. The knowledge required to do well on the test was the same knowledge required to evaluate whether you had done well. If you lacked the first, you necessarily lacked the second. Incompetence hides itself because recognizing incompetence requires the very competence you lack.

Since then, the effect has been demonstrated across domains. Medical students assessing their interviewing skills. Hunters evaluating their firearms knowledge. Debaters judging their argumentation quality. The pattern holds: low performers overestimate substantially, while high performers underestimate slightly.

But when AI collaboration enters the picture, something unexpected happens.

A 2025 study from Aalto University brought nearly 500 participants into the lab to complete difficult logical reasoning tasks from the Law School Admission Test. Half used large language models like ChatGPT. Half worked unaided. All participants took a test measuring their AI literacy, then estimated their own performance.

The researchers expected the classic Dunning-Kruger pattern: participants with low AI literacy would overestimate most dramatically, while those with high AI literacy would assess themselves more accurately. The data revealed the opposite.

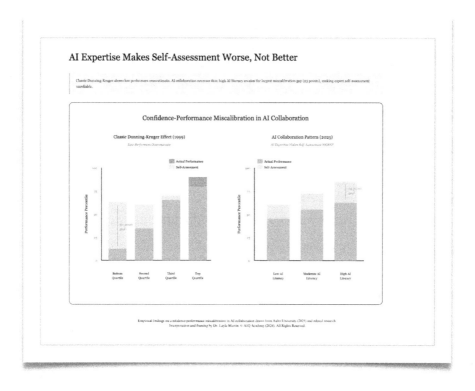

AI Expertise Makes Self-Assessment Worse, Not Better

Classic Dunning-Kruger shows low performers overestimate. AI collaboration reverses this: high AI literacy creates the largest miscalibration gap (23 points), making expert self-assessment unreliable.

Confidence-Performance Miscalibration in AI Collaboration

Classic Dunning-Kruger Effect (1999)
Low Performers Overestimate

AI Collaboration Pattern (2025)
AI Expertise Makes Self-Assessment WORSE

Empirical findings on confidence-performance miscalibration in AI collaboration drawn from Aalto University (2025) and related research. Interpretation and framing by Dr. Layla Martin © AIQ Academy (2026). All Rights Reserved.

The reversal is dramatic and counterintuitive.

In classic Dunning-Kruger studies from 1999, low performers show massive overestimation—the bottom quartile (12th percentile actual performance) estimated themselves at the 62nd percentile, a 50-point gap. As performance improves, self-assessment accuracy improves. The pattern slopes downward: incompetence creates the largest miscalibration.

179

But with AI collaboration, the pattern inverts. Aalto University's 2025 study measured 1,157 participants across three waves, controlling for IQ, social intelligence, AI literacy, and computer literacy. Participants with low AI literacy showed calibration errors. Participants with high AI literacy showed the largest miscalibration gap—23 percentage points.

This is a systematic reversal of a pattern documented across thousands of studies over decades.

Robin Welsch, the study's senior author, described the reversal bluntly: *"We would expect professionals who are AI literate to not only be a bit better at interacting with AI systems, but also at judging their performance with those systems. But this was not the case."*

The explanation appears to be cognitive offloading. When you delegate reasoning to an external system, you lose the internal feedback loop that would normally signal whether your thinking is sound. The AI produces fluent, confident-sounding output. You accept it and feel productive. You believe you have done good work. But you've outsourced the very cognitive processes that would allow you to evaluate quality.

The better you become at using AI, the more seamlessly you integrate its output into your thinking, the harder it becomes to distinguish your

1 person.
The output of 125.

The same task and quality criteria underwent a blind review by independent assessors. The same tools were available to all in the research study. What separated the participants was directional capability.

contribution from the tool's contribution—or to recognize where the tool has led you astray.

What this means for Creative Direction: The executive who feels most confident steering an AI-assisted strategy session may be the one contributing least to the actual direction. The confident feeling comes from the smooth operation of the tool, from outputs that sound authoritative, from a process that feels like leadership. Meanwhile, the fundamental choices—the conceptual architecture, the distinctive vision—are coming from the AI's training data patterns rather than from executive judgment.

For Synthesis Capability: Comprehensive documents that draw on multiple AI-generated analyses can feel like sophisticated integration. They cover many angles. They reference diverse sources. They look thorough. But synthesis is not aggregation. True synthesis creates coherence, finds the underlying unity, builds insight that transcends the component parts. What often emerges instead is a polished compilation where each section stands alone, where coverage substitutes for coherence.

For Iterative Refinement: The problem manifests as cycling without convergence. Multiple rounds of revision produce versions that differ without improving. The changes feel substantive because effort was invested and the AI generated alternatives. But version five is not

CROWDSOURCED PROFESSIONALS

ONE PERSON · DIRECTED AI COLLABORATION

One person with direction capability — iterative, intentional steering toward a held standard

125 professionals
Human experts, no AI assistance

1 person
Single individual with AI collaboration

2,520 hours
Combined labor investment

5.5 hours
Total time from start to final output

$2,555 cost
Crowdsourced labor fees

$27 cost
Total AI tool cost for the engagement

1 = 125

External evaluators, blind to which was which, rated the solo directed-AI output comparable or superior across every quality dimension measured — novelty, strategic viability, and real-world value. The tool was available to both. Directional capability was not.

measurably closer to excellence than version three. Activity has been confused with progress. Iteration without calibration becomes iteration without advancement.

Those most vulnerable to these patterns are least equipped to recognize them. Self-assessment requires the same capability being assessed. If your Creative Direction is weak, you cannot reliably judge whether your direction is weak. If your Synthesis Capability is limited, you cannot accurately evaluate whether you have achieved synthesis. The blind spot is structural, not correctable through introspection alone.

KEY INSIGHT: *Your Combined Intelligence Determines What AI Can Help You See*

There are many ways to improve your AIQ. But one that most discussions of AI literacy overlook is fundamental: you have to be smarter. Not in the credentialing sense. Smarter in the sense of having developed genuine intellectual depth and range.

This matters because AI amplifies what you bring to it. If you bring shallow thinking, you get shallow results wrapped in confident-sounding prose. If you bring limited knowledge, you cannot spot when the AI hallucinates historical facts or misrepresents reality. The quality of questions you can ask is bounded by what you understand.

The quality of answers you can recognize is bounded by what you know.

Consider hallucinations (not in terms of marijuana, LSD or psychedelic mushrooms). In this context, AI systems confidently describing events that never occurred, attributing quotes to wrong sources, inventing plausible-sounding details. If you lack sufficient

"I'm California sober, but I'm having trouble getting this done."

Fun fact. I was "raised" by hippies and intentionally named LSD, my initials at birth. To rebel, I read books. A lot of books… and was voted, *"Most Likely to Become a Librarian"* much to my parents' dismay. Los Angeles is a weird place because people say they're sober while micro-dosing mushrooms. I've never taken them. I guess it's called *California Sober*.

knowledge of history, of literature, of how the world truly works, you cannot catch these errors. They sound authoritative. They fit the pattern. They answer your question. You accept them and build your work on false foundations.

But someone who is genuinely well-read with depth across fields of study, spots the fabrication immediately. They know the historical timeline and recognize the misattributed quote. They catch the anachronism because the error violates their knowledge of reality.

The pattern is consistent: those with high AIQ tend to be genuinely well-read. They understand context and nuance and can draw on literature, philosophy, history, science. They possess cultural intelligence (CQ) that allows them to recognize what a question requires. They ask better questions because they have encountered more ideas, more ways of thinking, more frameworks for understanding complex problems. This is not coincidental.

Quality outputs depend entirely on quality questions. And the quality of your questions depends on the depth and breadth of what you have read. This means taking the time to read with sustained attention. Yes, I'm referring to holding a physical book in your hands. Not skimming articles, listening to audiobooks during commutes or watching YouTube summaries. Reading means engaging with text directly, at the pace thought requires, with the ability to pause, reflect and return.

Recent research tracking reading habits shows that only about 16 percent of Americans aged 15 and older read for pleasure every day, a steep decline of roughly 40 percent over the last 20 years. This is occurring even as attention spans shrink and quick digital summaries proliferate. This trend was documented in a large analysis of time-use data covering nearly 240,000 professionals, and it highlights how rare sustained, focused reading has become in modern life.

When so few professionals practice reading books regularly, its absence can explain why higher-order thinking and quality questioning feel thinner in many professional and creative spaces. Meaning, the work of developing AIQ begins long before you sit down with an AI system. It begins with how you build your own intellectual foundation.

This raises the uncomfortable question: if the blind spot is structural, and if development requires intellectual depth you may not have built yet, how do you even know where you stand? That question has no easy answer.

Chapter 11: Without Measurement

I started this book with an anomaly. Eighteen years of chess tournament data, more than six thousand matches, more than two thousand players, and buried inside those numbers was a pattern that refused to fit anything the researchers expected to find. The professionals who won were not the ones with the best chess skills or the most powerful computers. They were the ones who had learned how to direct the collaboration between the two.

That finding launched everything that followed. The researchers who traced that anomaly spent years building the rigorous case: that human-AI collaboration capability is real, that it is stable over time, that it is measurable, and that it is genuinely distinct from every other form of intelligence we had previously named. Something new that had always existed as a latent human capacity, waiting for the moment when the technology caught up to it.

That moment is now. And the question is do you know where you stand?

Not where you think you stand based on the confidence that comes from using AI regularly and producing work that seems better than without your AI tool, but where you measurably stand, observed from outside the fluency illusion that makes your AI output feel more capable than it is. The alternative to knowing is a gap that widens while you are unaware it exists.

In late 2025, a team of Stanford economists published findings from a comprehensive labor market study. They analyzed payroll records from more than 25 million American workers across tens of thousands of firms, tracking employment outcomes month by month as generative AI moved from novelty to infrastructure. What they found was an unexpected divergence between two groups: entry-level employment had declined in occupations where AI was automating work, while employment held and grew in occupations where AI was augmenting it.

The tools available to both groups were largely the same. The divergence came from how the human at the controls was using them.

THE FINDING THAT MATTERS

The tools available to both groups were largely the same. The divergence came entirely from how the human at the controls was using them. The tacit intelligence that tells you not just what to produce, but how to steer the process of producing it.

25M+	3 yrs	16%	0
American workers tracked via ADP payroll data	Monthly tracking, Oct 2022 through Sep 2025	Relative employment decline in highest AI-exposure roles, ages 22-25	No wage divergence detected. The gap is not arriving through your paycheck

WHY MOST PROFESSIONALS ARE THE LAST TO KNOW

✓ WHAT IS DIVERGING

Employment outcomes. Career trajectory. The accumulation of collaboration patterns that determine whether you are directing AI or being replaced by it.

✗ WHAT IS NOT DIVERGING

Salaries. The gap is not announcing itself through your paycheck. It is accumulating quietly, in outputs that sound fluent, in the comfortable sensation that you are using AI well because you are using it regularly.

The professionals most exposed to this divergence are, in most cases, the last to know.

Brynjolfsson, Chandar & Chen · Canaries in the Coal Mine? · Stanford Digital Economy Lab / NBER · Nov 2025 · Interpreted and applied to the AIQ framework by Dr. Layla Martin   AIQ™

Boussioux, L., Lane, J.N., Zhang, M., Jacimovic, V., & Lakhani, K.R. (2024). "The Crowdless Future? Generative AI and Creative Problem Solving." Harvard Business School Working Paper 24-005. Research interpretation by Layla Martin.

Further, what separated the two groups was the tacit intelligence that tells you not just what to produce but how to steer the process of producing it. The person who knows their area of expertise deeply, hands work to their AI tool and blankly accepts what comes back is in a different economic position than the person who uses that same expertise to direct what AI produces, challenge what it misses and synthesize what it generates into something that could only have come from them.

Here is the part of that study that should stay with you: the adjustment showing up in those labor markets is not visible in salaries. Wages have not diverged the way employment has. Which means there is no warning signal arriving through your paycheck. The gap is not announcing itself. Rather, it is accumulating quietly, in collaboration patterns that feel productive, in outputs that sound fluent, in the comfortable sensation that you are using AI well because you are using it regularly. The professionals most exposed to this divergence are, in most cases, the last to know. That is the present condition for the majority of professionals today.

Now, consider what Harvard Business School researchers found when they studied what the high-end of directed collaboration produces: one person, working with an AI tool for five and a half hours, at a cost of twenty-seven dollars, generated results that were comparable or superior across every quality dimension to what previously required

125 professionals, 2,520 hours, and $2,555 worth of crowdsourced labor. The study measured novelty. It measured strategic viability and real-world value. In every dimension that mattered, directed human-AI collaboration matched or exceeded what a room full of professionals produced without it.

Take a moment with that number. One person = one hundred and twenty-five professionals. The same output, measured by external evaluators who did not know which was which. The tool was available to everyone. So, it was not the AI that created that gap. It was the direction capability of the person at the controls, the iterative and intentional steering that shaped what was possible, that pushed past the first adequate answer, that held the work to a standard the tool alone would never have reached.

That is the range this chapter is asking you to locate yourself within. On one end, effort that plateaus and on the other, a single person producing what previously required a room. Both feel like work and productivity. The difference is not visible from inside your own experience of using AI. It only becomes legible when you have something external to measure against. Without measurement, you have no way of knowing whether you are the person who turns five hours into the output of 125, or whether you are one of the 125 being replaced.

Yes, professionals who collaborate effectively with AI are working faster. But there's more than that: they are completing categories of work that others will not be able to conceptualize, let alone execute. The difference is not incremental improvement in speed or quality. It is closer to an order of magnitude difference in leverage. When collaboration is refined across all five dimensions, effort compounds. When it is not, effort plateaus. And that gap does not stay small. It widens, quietly, without announcing itself, in the space between what you are producing and what you do not yet know is possible.

You cannot close a gap you cannot see.

Without that clarity, you are practicing in the dark. Investing effort without knowing whether you are developing the capability that matters or simply getting better at something you are already good enough at.

With it, you have something most professionals lack. Accurate data about where you stand and a precise target for what to develop next. This is a serious moment in how work gets done. It is also a moment of extraordinary possibility for those willing to see themselves clearly. The guarantees are gone. The patterns are visible. The divergence has already begun.

Chapter 11: The Choice Ahead

In the sweltering July summer of 1799, a twenty-eight-year-old French lieutenant named Pierre-François Bouchard was occupied with the monotonous physics of survival. His orders were to strengthen the defences of Fort Julien. Built on the ruins of a fifteenth-century Mamluk stronghold on the left bank of the Nile, Fort Julien was positioned to guard the river's approach from the Mediterranean against British and Ottoman naval incursions. The fort sat roughly six kilometers northeast of the port city of Rosetta (modern day Rashid) and the garrison defending it numbered roughly two hundred and sixty men.

The men were poorly supplied, suffering from ophthalmia and dysentery, working in Egyptian summer heat with the knowledge that an Ottoman assault could arrive by sea at any moment. Napoleon's Army of the Orient was overextended and slowly losing its grip on Egypt. Under Bouchard's command, a small detachment of sappers and infantrymen had been assigned the particular misery of demolishing an old interior wall. It was the rough kind of work that produces rubble, blisters, and nothing else.

To most of those men, the earth was simply a medium for barricades, and the stones within it were merely heavy things to be stacked or discarded. But as the soldiers demolished an interior wall of the fort, their tools struck a slab of granodiorite that refused to be ignored. It was soot-colored, jagged, and entirely unremarkable to the eye that sought only a sturdier fortification. Bouchard had every practical reason to press on. He had walls to reinforce and a war to survive. Instead, he made the quiet, almost infinitesimal choice to pause. He examined the stone. Beneath the grime of centuries, he recognized a rhythm: the distinct, mathematical repetition of three different scripts etched into the dark face of the rock. The stone revealed Ancient Greek, Demotic, and Egyptian hieroglyphs, all layered one beneath the other like voices in a chord.

In that moment of stillness, Bouchard did something that would take scholars another twenty-three years to complete. He understood that he was looking at a key. While he could read none of the three scripts, he required no expertise to understand the gravity of what he had discovered. In that moment, Bouchard was willing to look at a plain stone in a pile of discards and ask whether it might be something more.

For fourteen centuries, the written record of one of history's greatest civilizations had been sitting in plain view. It was chiseled into temple walls, painted on tomb ceilings, pressed into papyrus waiting for someone to recognize it as language rather than decoration. The knowledge was present the entire time but the capacity to decode it simply had to be chosen. History, we are often told, is made by the swing of the sword. More often, it is preserved by those who take the time to look closer at what most skip over.

The shift I've described, the blurring of lines between human intent and machine execution, could be viewed as our own Nile Delta. Most professionals are currently busy building walls. They are reacting to the sheer weight of the technology, trying to stack skills or discard old habits just to keep the fort standing and treating AI as a heavy object to be managed rather than a system to be read. The result is that they are exhausting themselves rearranging stones while the real discovery lies just beneath their feet. Buried within this transition is the small choice to stop and measure the underlying patterns of your own intelligence. The choice to ask how you personally collaborate with AI.

The five dimensions we have uncovered: Creative Direction, Emotional Translation, Analytical Partnership, Synthesis Capability, and Iterative Refinement, are the specific channels through which the gap between you and your highest-potential work either opens or closes every day. They are the behavioral signatures that appear, consistently and measurably, in the transcripts of professionals who collaborate well with AI and in those who believe they do.

The historical figures at the center of this book were each, in their own time, doing something that looked from the outside like ordinary work. Cleopatra staging a diplomatic meeting. Gibran writing letters from a rented room in New York. Hume revising a book that had failed. Rikyū arranging a tea room. Meitner doing calculations that no one yet understood would matter. What distinguished them was a particular quality of engagement: the capacity to shape the intelligence available to them rather than simply receive it, to direct output rather than accept it, to iterate toward precision rather than settle for coherence.

That capacity is the opportunity to develop, or, more precisely, to discover whether you already have it, and in which directions it wants to grow.

Bouchard's predecessors walked past discoveries like the Rosetta Stone for decades. They were, by every measure, intelligent and capable people. They simply had no framework for recognizing what a key looked like from the outside, and nothing in the appearance of a soot-colored slab of granodiorite told them to stop. You stop when you understand what you are looking for. You understand what you are looking for only when you recognize the pattern.

If the work of developing AIQ begins with your intellectual foundation, then the AIQ Assessment could be considered your personal Rosetta Stone.

You are currently standing in front of a wall of technology that is moving faster than any individual's ability to intuit their own

relationship to it. The choice ahead is whether you will remain the soldier building the wall, managing the weight of the technology with practiced effort and diminishing returns, or become the person who pauses to examine what the stone is trying to reveal. Bouchard required no expertise in ancient languages to recognize that he was looking at a key. He needed only the willingness to stop when everyone else was moving, to kneel in the dust and look closer at what the moment was offering.

The stone is in front of you now. The next question is what action will you take?

T hank you for reading AIQ 2026! You recognize that the old rules of working are dissolving. You don't need a boss, nor do you want to be part of the online-job-search-engagement-theater, where your expertise is performed for an algorithm.

AIQ Ninja is a dojo for augmented intelligence. It is designed to help you protect your time, and monetize your expertise through proven capability. Our mission is to cultivate refined AIQ in one hundred million people—practitioners who choose evidence over intuition to reclaim their agency.

- *Step 1:* **Baseline** (White Headband) Take the U.S. Patent Pending AIQ Assessment at aiqninja.com. This is your prerequisite. It provides you with a data-backed baseline of your collaborative intelligence.

- *Step 2:* **Refinement** (Maven Course Certification) Don't waste your time on what you already know. Use your AIQ Assessment scores to enter targeted, one-week intensives. You sharpen the specific dimensions needed to turn your expertise into high-leverage value.

- *Step 3:* **Leverage** (Black Headband) Once you reach mastery, you don't post to be found. You are welcomed into our **AIQ Directory**, a professional showcase that allows you to monetize your proven skills directly with those who need them.

- *Step 4:* **Legacy** (Publishing & Podcast) Launch your voice and your brand through **The AIQ Ninja Collective**. By utilizing our publishing imprint and podcast network, you aren't building your brand alone. Join our like-minded community to transform your expertise into a monetized asset, build your authority, and empower others to do the same.

- Begin at aiqninja.com

About the Author

D
r. Layla Martin is a featured expert at the intersection of sense-making and systems. Her research explores how we see and interact with the unknown—from how humans prioritize and interact with outer space, to the history of information suppression during the Scottish witch trials (1563-1736).

Before re-entering academia, Martin was a Creative Director at Warner Bros. Entertainment Inc., where she oversaw the international art servicing for the *Harry Potter* and *Lord of the Rings* franchises across 32 countries.

Having earned her Master's from Harvard University and completed Executive Education at Yale School of Management and MIT Sloan, Martin chose a non-traditional path for her doctorate to escape the rigidity of the Ivory Tower. Her research traces how knowledge is controlled, from the Scottish Witch Trials to the 2020's, uncovering who, most often, is left out of the narrative.

Highlights of Martin's featured work include *Harvard University Magazine* and *The Space Review*. As a nominated member of the Conference of the Parties (COP26), she worked to connect global leaders with the understanding that outer space is also an environment in need of protection. Through The Layla Martin Foundation (est. 2012) Martin has personally funded over 180 loans to women entrepreneurs without access to traditional capital.

Martin's previous book, *AIQ The Pattern in the Noise,* ranked #1 on Amazon. *AIQ 2026* is the culmination of a career spent questioning the motivation behind the "system" and how to thrive when it was built neither by you nor for you.

On Substack, Martin invites you to *"Read like it's 1999. Think like it's 2029."* She shares intelligence in all its forms—ranging from high-tech to historical, including insight on human evolution in 2026+. You can find Layla Martin at aiqninja.com.

AIQ 2026 - Works Cited

Chapter 1

Ang, Soon, and Linn Van Dyne. *Handbook of Cultural Intelligence: Theory, Measurement, and Applications*. Routledge, 2008.

Ang, Soon, et al. "Cultural Intelligence: Its Measurement and Effects on Cultural Judgment and Decision Making, Cultural Adaptation, and Task Performance." *Management and Organization Review*, vol. 3, no. 3, 2007, pp. 335–371.

Binet, Alfred, and Théodore Simon. *Méthodes nouvelles pour le diagnostic du niveau intellectuel des anormaux*. L'Année Psychologique, 1905.

Brysbaert, Marc. "Two Persistent Myths About Binet and the Origins of Intelligence Testing." *Collabra: Psychology*, vol. 10, no. 1, 2024, Article 117600, https://online.ucpress.edu/collabra/article/10/1/117600.

Cavallo, Kathleen, and Donna Brienza. *Emotional Competence and Leadership Excellence at Johnson & Johnson*. Hay/McBer Group, commissioned report, 1998.

ChessBase. "Dark Horse ZackS Wins Freestyle Chess Tournament." *ChessBase*, 19 June 2005.

Earley, P. Christopher, and Soon Ang. *Cultural Intelligence: Individual Interactions Across Cultures*. Stanford University Press, 2003.

Ferry, Jules. *Loi du 28 mars 1882 sur l'enseignement primaire obligatoire*. République Française.

Goleman, Daniel. *Emotional Intelligence: Why It Can Matter More Than IQ*. Bantam Books, 1995.

Kasparov, Garry. "The Chess Master and the Computer." *The New York Review of Books*, 11 Feb. 2010. MIT OpenCourseWare reprint.

Nicolas, Serge, et al. "Sick? Or Slow? On the Origins of Intelligence as a Psychological Object." *Intelligence*, vol. 41, no. 5, 2013, pp. 699–711, https://doi.org/10.1016/j.intell.2013.08.006.

Qin, Xin, Jackson G. Lu, et al. "Artificial Intelligence Quotient (AIQ): Measuring Human–AI Collaborative Intelligence." *SSRN Electronic Journal*, 2024.

Salovey, Peter, and John D. Mayer. "Emotional Intelligence." *Imagination, Cognition and Personality*, vol. 9, no. 3, 1990, pp. 185–211.

Stern, William. *Die psychologischen Methoden der Intelligenzprüfung*. Barth, 1912.

Terman, Lewis M. *The Measurement of Intelligence*. Houghton Mifflin, 1916.

Chapter 2

Caruso, David. "Defining the Inkblot Called Emotional Intelligence." Consortium for Research on Emotional Intelligence in Organizations, https://www.eiconsortium.org/reprints/ ei_issues_and_common_misunderstandings_caruso_comment.html.

Cavallo K, Brienza D (2001). "Emotional Competence and Leadership Excellence at Johnson & Johnson: The Emotional Intelligence and Leadership Study". *Consortium for Research on Emotional Intelligence in Organizations*.

Challenger, Gray & Christmas, Inc. Job Cut Announcement Report: 2025 Year-End Review. Challenger, Gray & Christmas, 2025, https://www.challengergray.com.

Davies, Michèle, Lazar Stankov, and Richard D. Roberts. "Emotional Intelligence: In Search of an Elusive Construct." Journal of

Personality and Social Psychology, vol. 75, no. 4, 1998, pp. 989–1015.

Davis, Gerald F. "What Might Replace the Modern Corporation?" Harvard Business Review, July–Aug. 2023, https://hbr.org/2023/07/what-might-replace-the-modern-corporation.

International Labour Organization. *Global Employment Trends for Youth 2024*: Decent Work, Brighter Futures. ILO, 2024.

Jassy, Andy. "Shareholder Letter." Amazon.com, Inc. Annual Report, 2023, https://www.aboutamazon.com/investor-relations.

Johnson, Richard W., and Barbara A. Butrica. *The Finanical Consequences of Job Loss after Age 50*. Urban Institute, 2012, www.urban.org/sites/default/files/publication/25441/412588-The-Financial-Consequences-of-Job-Loss-after-Age--.PDF.

Locke, Edwin A. "Why Emotional Intelligence Is an Invalid Concept." Journal of Organizational Behavior, vol. 26, no. 4, 2005, pp. 425–431.

Matthews, Gerald, Moshe Zeidner, and Richard D. Roberts. Emotional Intelligence: Science and Myth. MIT Press, 2002.

Mayer, John D., Peter Salovey, and David R. Caruso. Mayer-Salovey-Caruso Emotional Intelligence Test (MSCEIT). Multi-Health Systems, 2002.

Microsoft Corporation. Form 8-K and Earnings Call Transcripts. Microsoft Investor Relations, 2024–2025, https://www.microsoft.com/investor.

Papadopoulos, Michael, et al. *Older Workers Face Higher Risk of Mid-Career Unemployment Than Previously Known*. Schwartz Center for Economic Policy Analysis (SCEPA), 2020.

Salesforce, Inc. Q4 FY2024 Earnings Call Transcript. Salesforce Investor Relations, 2024, https://investor.salesforce.com.

Salovey, Peter, and John D. Mayer. "Emotional Intelligence." Imagination, Cognition and Personality, vol. 9, no. 3, 1990, pp. 185–211, https://doi.org/10.2190/DUGG-P24E-52WK-6CDG.

World Economic Forum. The Future of Jobs Report 2023. World Economic Forum, 2023, https://www.weforum.org/publications/the-future-of-jobs-report-2023.

World Economic Forum. The Future of Jobs Report 2025. World Economic Forum, 2025, https://www.weforum.org/reports/the-future-of-jobs-report-2025.

Chapter 3

National Institute of Neurological Disorders and Stroke. "Parkinson's Disease: Hope Through Research." National Institutes of Health, 2 Mar. 2020, www.ninds.nih.gov/publications/parkinsons-disease-hope-through-research.

National Institute of Neurological Disorders and Stroke. "Parkinson's Disease: Hope Through Research." National Institutes of Health, PDF, www.ninds.nih.gov/sites/default/files/2025-05/parkinsons-disease-hope-through-research.pdf.

"History of the Building." German Watch Museum Glashütte, Stiftung Deutsches Uhrenmuseum Glashütte, www.uhrenmuseum-glashuette.com/en/exhibitions/history-of-the-building/.

"AI and LinkedIn Applications." *The New York Times*, DealBook, 21 June 2025.

Uhrmacherschule Glashütte. "Uhrmacherschule Glashütte." Deutsche Uhrmacherschule Glashütte, uhrmacherschule-glashuette.de/.

Fondation de la Haute Horlogerie. "Seamaster 1948 Limited Edition
by Omega." *Fondation de la Haute Horlogerie*,
www.hautehorlogerie.org/en/watches-and-culture/watchmaking-
scene/watches-and-novelties/seamaster-1948-limited-edition.

Chapter 4

Remington, Frederic. *The Right of the Road.* 1900, oil on canvas.
Amon Carter Museum of American Art, Fort Worth, Texas,
https://www.cartermuseum.org/collection/right-road-1985-66.

Herlihy, David V. "How the Bicycle Changed History." *Smithsonian
Magazine*, Smithsonian Institution,
https://www.smithsonianmag.com/history/how-the-bicycle-changed-
history-6275551/.

Dunning, David, and Justin Kruger. "Unskilled and Unaware of It:
How Difficulties in Recognizing One's Own Incompetence Lead to
Inflated Self-Assessments." *Journal of Personality and Social
Psychology*, vol. 77, no. 6, 1999, pp. 1121–1134.

Chapter 5

Plutarch. *Life of Antony.* Translated by Bernadotte Perrin, Harvard
University Press, 1920. *Loeb Classical Library*,

www.perseus.tufts.edu/hopper/text?
doc=Perseus%3Atext%3A2008.01.0006.

Plutarch. *The Parallel Lives*. Translated by John Dryden, revised by
Arthur Hugh Clough, Modern Library, 2001.

Roller, Duane W. *Cleopatra: A Biography*. Oxford University Press,
2010.

Goldsworthy, Adrian. *Antony and Cleopatra*. Yale University Press,
2010.

Hölbl, Günther. *A History of the Ptolemaic Empire*. Routledge, 2001.

Grant, Michael. *Cleopatra*. Phoenix Press, 2000.

Chapter 6

Bushrui, Suheil B., and Joe Jenkins. *Kahlil Gibran: Man and Poet*.
Oneworld Publications, 1998.

Gibran, Khalil. *The Prophet*. Alfred A. Knopf, 1923.

Haskell, Mary, and Khalil Gibran. *Beloved Prophet: The Love Letters
of Khalil Gibran and Mary Haskell*. Edited by Virginia Hilu, Alfred
A. Knopf, 1972.

Chapter 7

Hume, David. *A Treatise of Human Nature: Being an Attempt to Introduce the Experimental Method of Reasoning into Moral Subjects*. Printed for John Noon, 1739–1740. Project Gutenberg, www.gutenberg.org/ebooks/4705.

Hume, David. *An Enquiry Concerning Human Understanding*. 1748. Edited by Tom L. Beauchamp, Oxford University Press, 1999.

Hume, David. "My Own Life." *The Life of David Hume, Esq. Written by Himself*, printed for W. Strahan and T. Cadell, 1777. Econlib, www.econlib.org/library/LFBooks/Hume/hmMOL.html.

Mossner, Ernest Campbell. *The Life of David Hume*. 2nd ed., Oxford University Press, 2001, pp. 154–156.

Norton, David Fate. "The Bibliothèque raisonnée Review of Hume's Treatise." *Hume Studies*, vol. 32, no. 2, 2006, pp. 315–347.

Ramsay, Allan. *David Hume, 1711–1776. Historian and Philosopher*. 1754. National Galleries of Scotland, www.nationalgalleries.org/art-and-artists/60610/david-hume-1711-1776-historian-and-philosopher-1754.

Bibliothèque raisonnée des ouvrages des savants de l'Europe. Vol. 19, 1740.

Chapter 8

Anonymous. *Portrait of Sen no Rikyū*. Momoyama period, late 16th century. Kyoto National Museum, Kyoto.

Koren, Leonard. *Wabi-Sabi for Artists, Designers, Poets & Philosophers.* Imperfect Publishing, 1994.

Kuck, Loraine E. *The Art of Japanese Gardens.* Crown Publishers, 1968.

Murata, Shukō. *Shukō Meibutsu-ki* [*Records of the Tea Gathering*]. 15th century. Translated excerpts in Sen, Sōshitsu XV, *The Japanese Way of Tea.* University of Hawai'i Press, 1998.

Pitelka, Morgan. *Japanese Tea Culture: Art, History, and Practice.* Routledge, 2003.

Rikyū, Sen no. *Rikyū Hyakkaijō* [*One Hundred Rules of Tea*]. 16th century. Translated excerpts in Sen, Sōshitsu XV, *The Japanese Way of Tea.* University of Hawai'i Press, 1998.

Sen, Sōshitsu XV. *The Japanese Way of Tea: From Its Origins in China to Sen Rikyū.* University of Hawai'i Press, 1998.

Varley, H. Paul. *Japanese Culture.* 4th ed., University of Hawai'i Press, 2000.

Yanagi, Sōetsu. *The Unknown Craftsman: A Japanese Insight into Beauty.* Kodansha International, 1989.

Chapter 9

Bernstein, Jeremy. *Hitler's Uranium Club: The Secret Recordings at Farm Hall.* Springer, 2001.

Bohr, Niels. "Neutron Capture and Nuclear Constitution." *Nature*, vol. 137, no. 3476, 1936, pp. 344–348. https://doi.org/10.1038/137344a0.

Einstein, Albert. "Does the Inertia of a Body Depend upon Its Energy Content?" *Annalen der Physik*, vol. 18, 1905, pp. 639–641. English translation in *The Principle of Relativity*, translated by W. Perrett and G. B. Jeffery, Dover Publications, 1952.

Frisch, Otto R. "Physical Evidence for the Division of Heavy Nuclei under Neutron Bombardment." *Nature*, vol. 143, no. 3616, 1939, pp. 276–276. https://doi.org/10.1038/143276a0.

Gamow, George. "The Liquid Drop Model of the Atomic Nucleus." *Journal of Physics*, vol. 51, 1931, pp. 204–212.

Hahn, Otto, and Fritz Strassmann. "Über den Nachweis und das Verhalten der bei der Bestrahlung des Urans mittels Neutronen entstehenden Erdalkalimetalle." *Naturwissenschaften*, vol. 27, no. 1, 1939, pp. 11–15.

Meitner, Lise, and Otto R. Frisch. "Disintegration of Uranium by Neutrons: A New Type of Nuclear Reaction." *Nature*, vol. 143, no. 3615, 1939, pp. 239–240.

Pais, Abraham. *Inward Bound: Of Matter and Forces in the Physical World*. Oxford University Press, 1986.

Sime, Ruth Lewin. *Lise Meitner: A Life in Physics*. University of California Press, 1996.

Walker, Mark. *German National Socialism and the Quest for Nuclear Power, 1939–1949*. Cambridge University Press, 1989.

Chapter 10

Buçinca, Zana, Maja Barbara Bruun, and Kasper Hornbæk. "Trust, But Verify: The Effects of AI Transparency on Human Decision-Making." *Proceedings of the 2021 CHI Conference on Human Factors in Computing Systems*, ACM, 2021.

Dunning, David, and Justin Kruger. "Unskilled and Unaware of It: How Difficulties in Recognizing One's Own Incompetence Lead to Inflated Self-Assessments." *Journal of Personality and Social Psychology*, vol. 77, no. 6, 1999, pp. 1121–1134.

Gigerenzer, Gerd. *Risk Savvy: How to Make Good Decisions*. Viking, 2014.

Kahneman, Daniel. *Thinking, Fast and Slow*. Farrar, Straus and Giroux, 2011.

Kruger, Justin, and David Dunning. "Unskilled and Unaware—But Why? A Reply to Krueger and Mueller." *Journal of Personality and Social Psychology*, vol. 85, no. 2, 2003, pp. 219–224.

Parker, Emily. "American Reading Habits Show Steep Decline as Digital Distractions Grow." *The Washington Post*, 20 Aug. 2025,

van den Bosch, Karel, et al. "Overconfidence and Under-Reliance in Human–AI Decision Making." *IEEE Transactions on Human-Machine Systems*, vol. 53, no. 1, 2023, pp. 45–56. https://doi.org/10.1109/THMS.2022.3213456.

Welsch, Robin, et al. "Artificial Intelligence Literacy Can Increase Overconfidence in Human–AI Collaboration." *Proceedings of the ACM on*

Human-Computer Interaction, vol. 9, no. CSCW1, 2025, Article 32. https://doi.org/10.1145/3637374.

Welsch, Robin. Quoted in Aalto University press release, "AI Literacy Does Not Improve Self-Assessment Accuracy in AI-Assisted Reasoning Tasks." Aalto University, 2025.

Chapter 11

Brynjolfsson, Erik, Bharat Chandar, and Ruyu Chen. "Canaries in the Coal Mine? Six Facts about the Recent Employment Effects of Artificial Intelligence." Stanford Digital Economy Lab Working Paper, 13 November 2025.

Boussioux, Léonard, Jacqueline N. Lane, Miaomiao Zhang, Vladimir Jacimovic, and Karim R. Lakhani. "The Crowdless Future? Generative AI and Creative Problem Solving." Harvard Business School Working Paper No. 24-005, 2024.

Chapter 12

Adkins, Lesley, and R. A. Adkins. *The Keys of Egypt: The Obsession to Decipher Egyptian Hieroglyphs*. HarperCollins, 2000.

Meyerson, Daniel. *The Linguist and the Emperor: Napoleon and Champollion's Quest to Decipher the Rosetta Stone*. Ballantine Books, 2004.

Solé, Robert, and Dominique Valbelle. *The Rosetta Stone: The Story of the Decoding of Hieroglyphics*. Four Walls Eight Windows, 2002.

www.ingramcontent.com/pod-product-compliance
Lightning Source LLC
LaVergne TN
LVHW081524050326
832903LV00025B/1619